# Non-verbal Reasoning

## 10 Minute Tests

### 9–10 years

# Test 1: Identifying Shapes

Test time: 0 ... 5 ... 10 minutes

Which is the odd one out?

*Example*

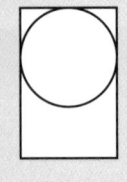  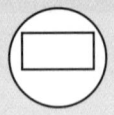 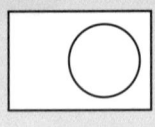 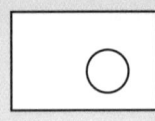
    a              b              ©              d              e

**1**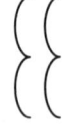
  a              b              c              d              e

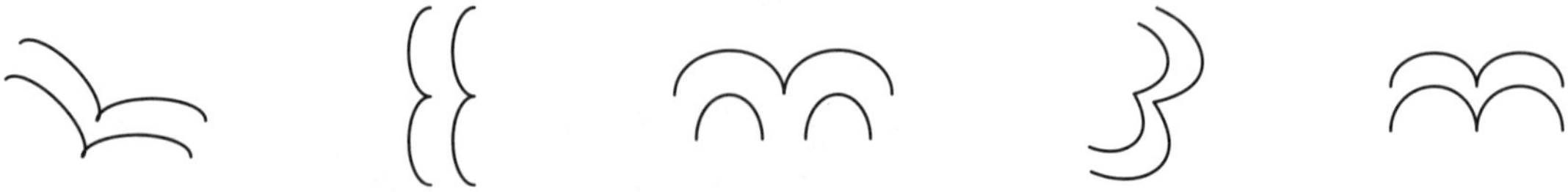

**2**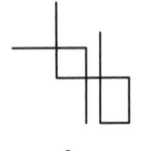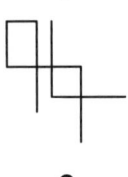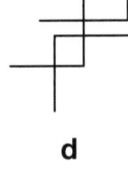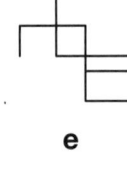
  a              b              c              d              e

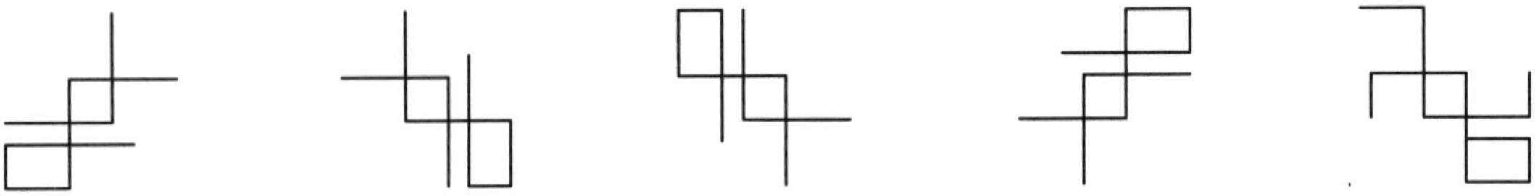

**3**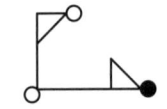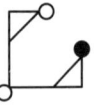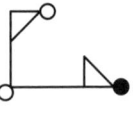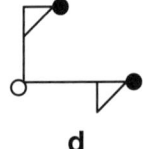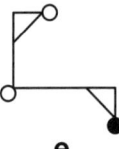
  a              b              c              d              e

**4**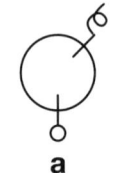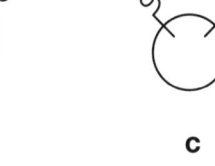

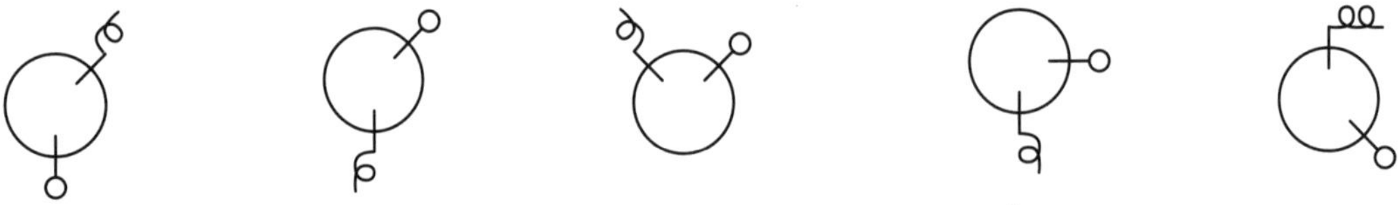

**5**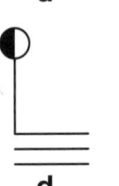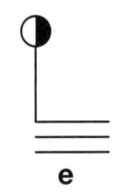
  a              b              c              d              e

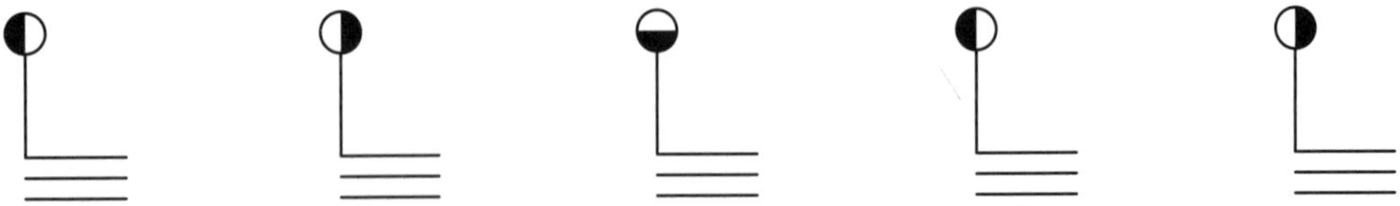

**6**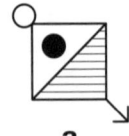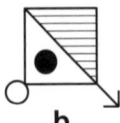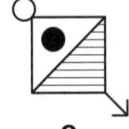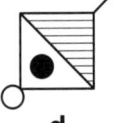
  a              b              c              d              e

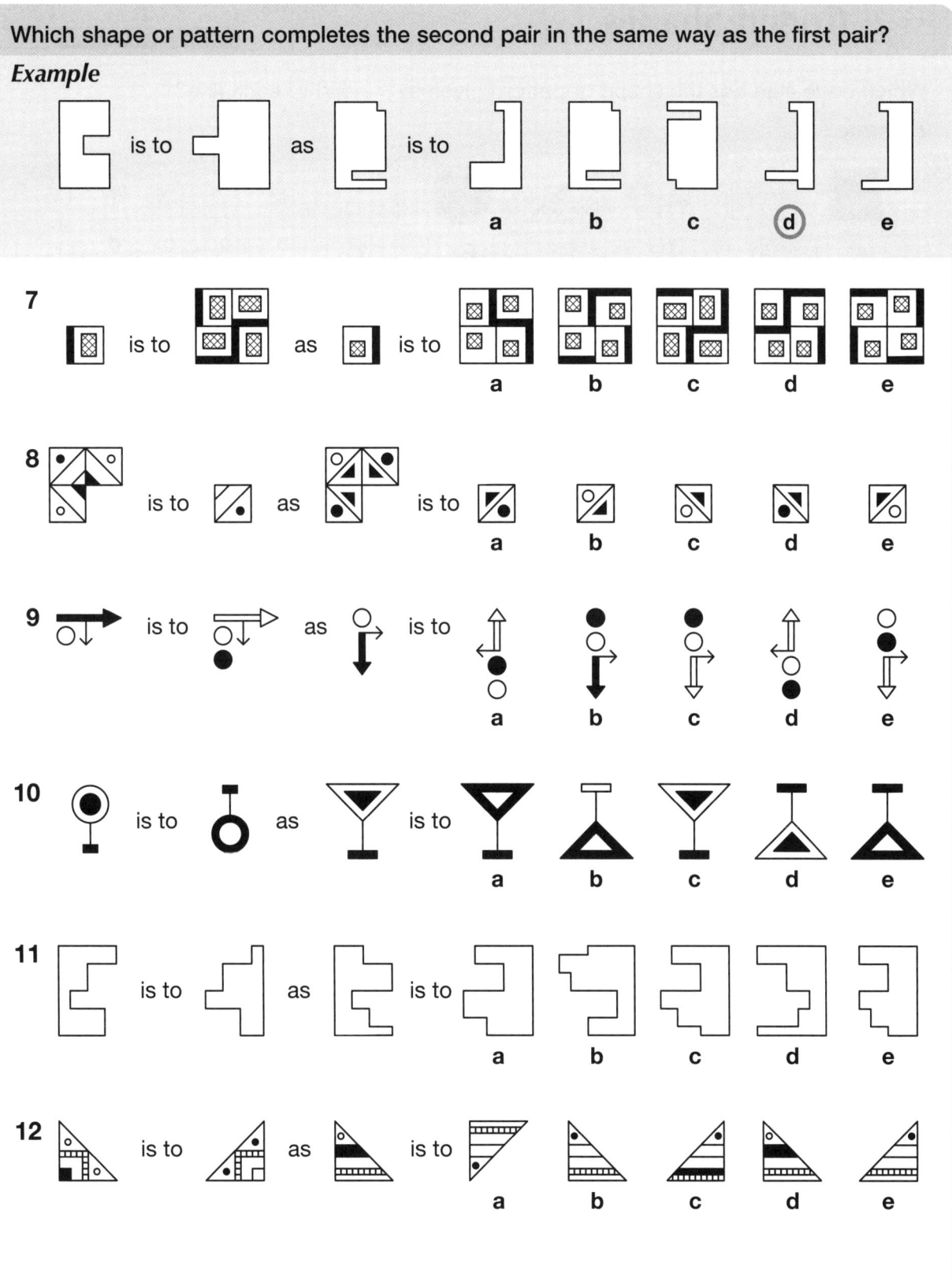

# TEST 2: Coded Shapes

Test time: 0 — 5 — 10 minutes

Which code matches the shape or pattern given at the end of each line?

*Example*

| | | | | | | BZ | AZ | CX | BY | CZ |
|---|---|---|---|---|---|---|---|---|---|---|
| AX | AY | BZ | CY | BX | ? | a | b | c | d | (e) |

**1**

| | | | | | | AY | CZ | BX | AX | DZ |
|---|---|---|---|---|---|---|---|---|---|---|
| AZ | CY | DX | BY | BZ | ? | a | b | c | d | e |

**2**

| | | | | | | MG | LF | MD | NE | ND |
|---|---|---|---|---|---|---|---|---|---|---|
| LE | NG | ME | NF | LD | ? | a | b | c | d | e |

**3**

| | | | | | | CX | BX | AY | AX | CZ |
|---|---|---|---|---|---|---|---|---|---|---|
| BY | BZ | CX | CY | AZ | ? | a | b | c | d | e |

**4**

| | | | | | | AY | DW | CX | AW | BX |
|---|---|---|---|---|---|---|---|---|---|---|
| CZ | BY | DX | AZ | CW | ? | a | b | c | d | e |

**5**

| | | | | | | JQ | MR | KS | MP | JS |
|---|---|---|---|---|---|---|---|---|---|---|
| JP | KQ | LR | LP | KR | MS | ? | a | b | c | d | e |

**6**

| | | | | | | EQ | GR | ER | FP | DR |
|---|---|---|---|---|---|---|---|---|---|---|
| GQ | DP | EP | FQ | FR | DQ | ? | a | b | c | d | e |

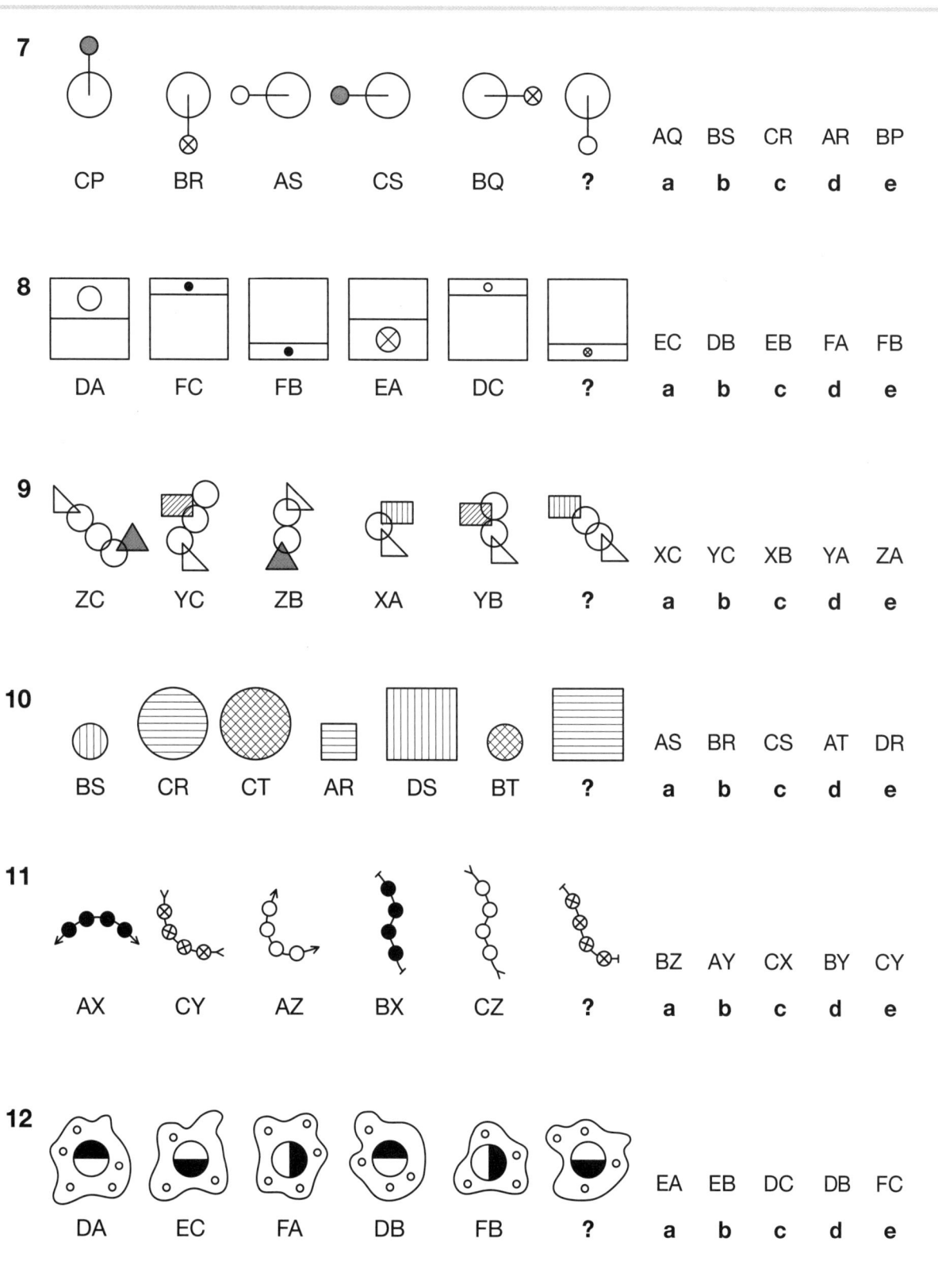

# TEST 3: Identifying Shapes

Which is the odd one out?

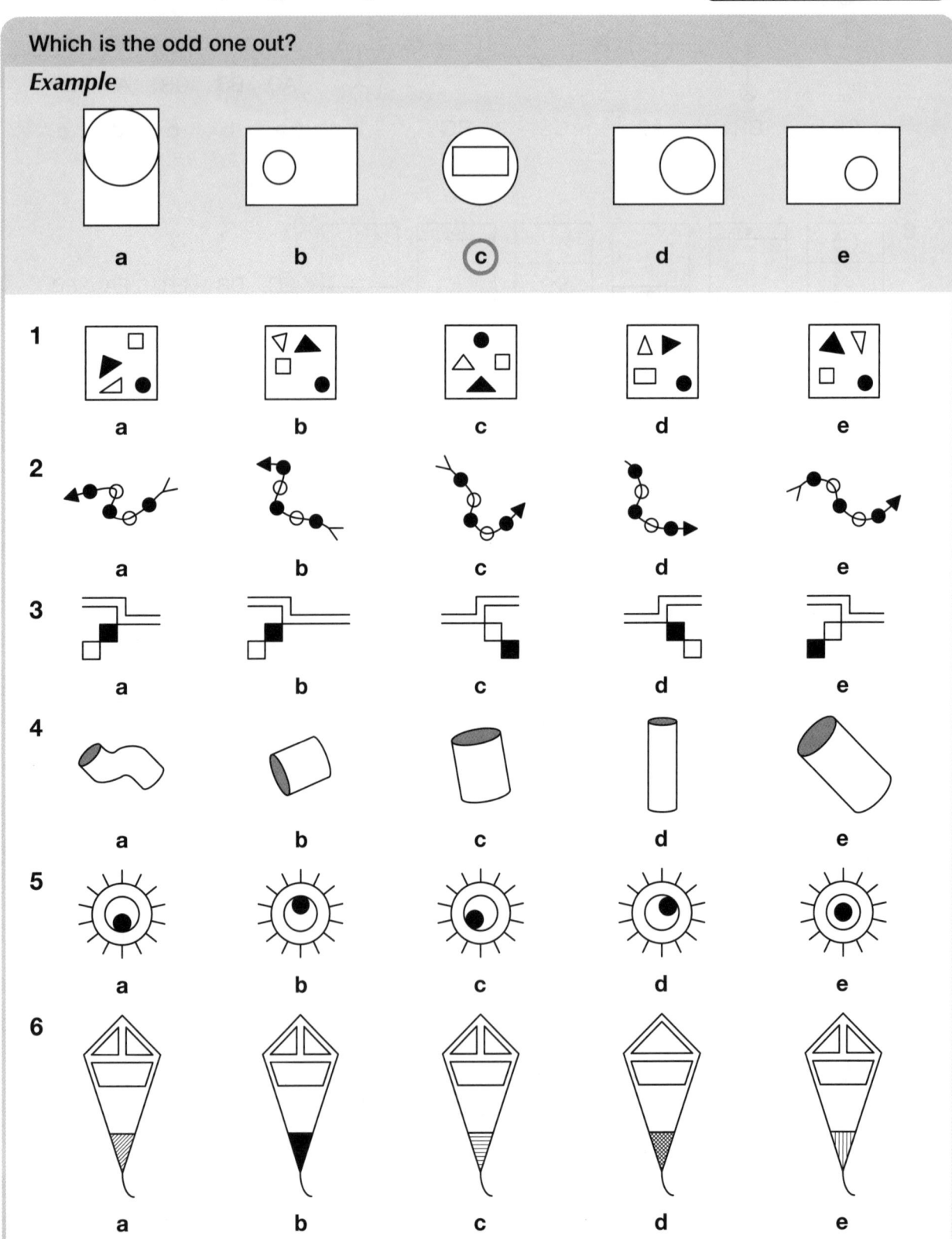

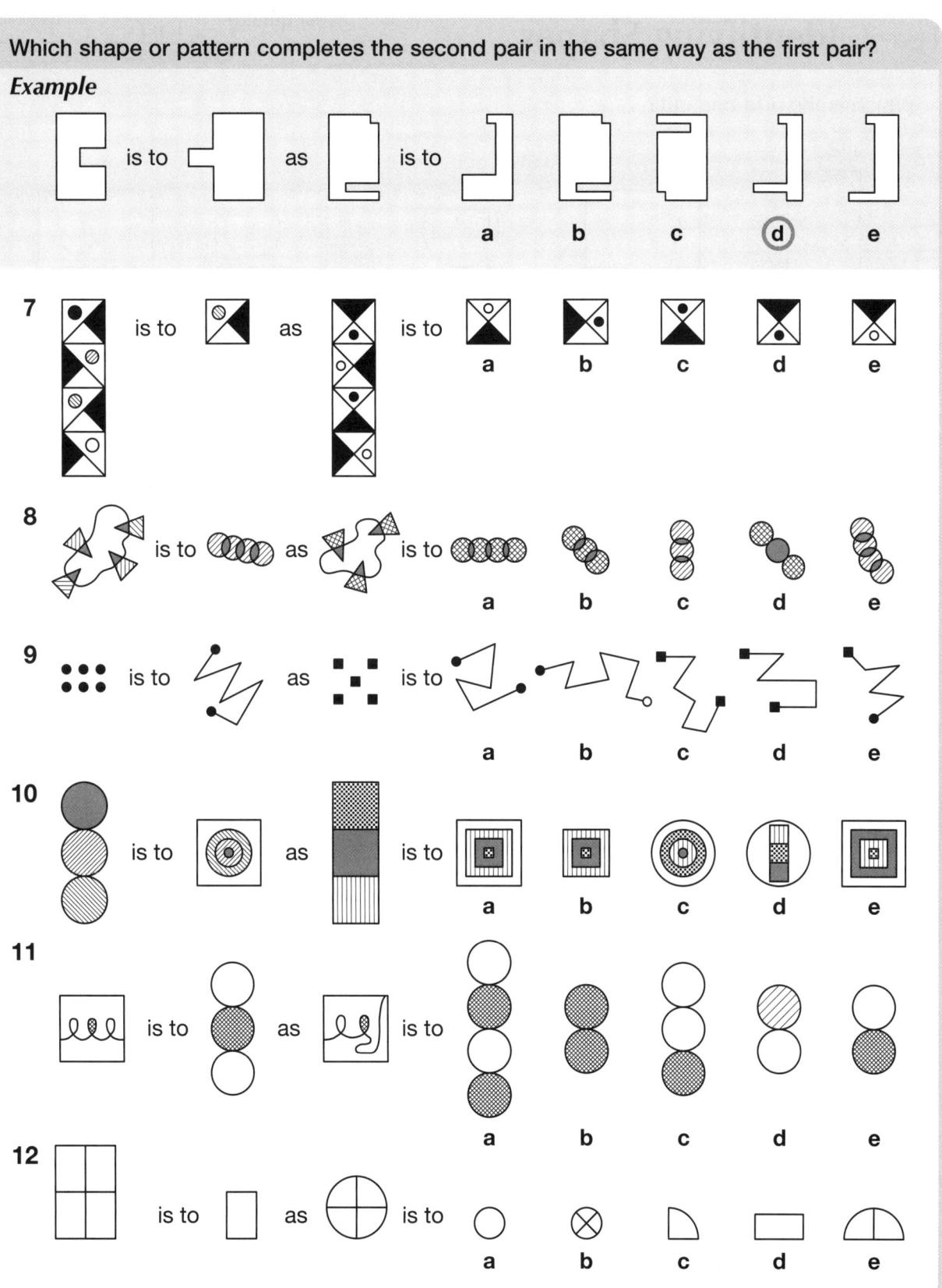

TEST 4: **Identifying Shapes**

Test time: 0　　5　　10 minutes

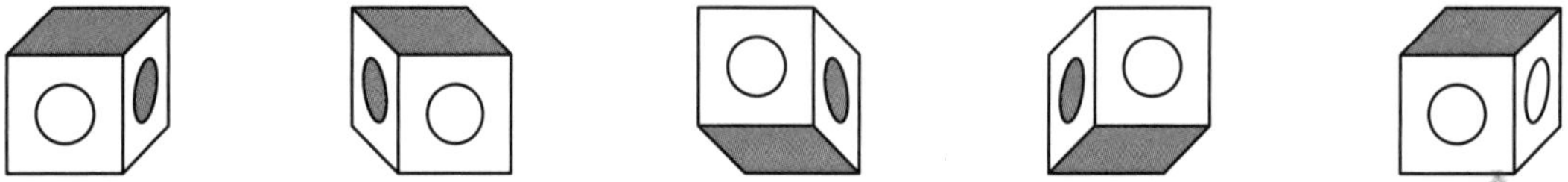

Which is the odd one out?

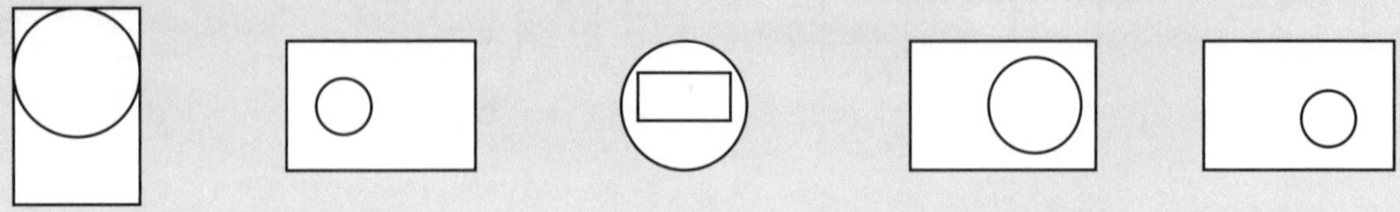

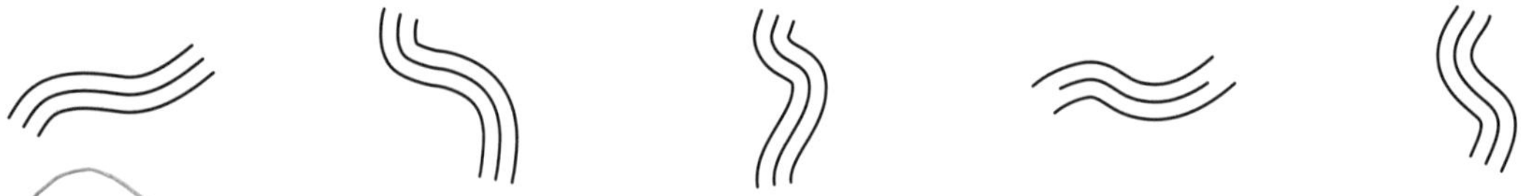

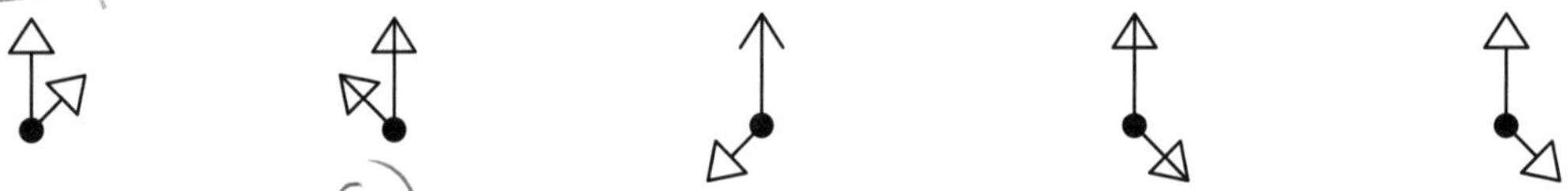

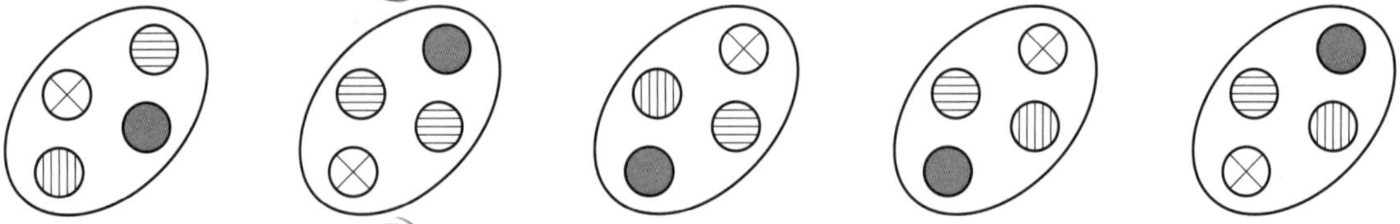

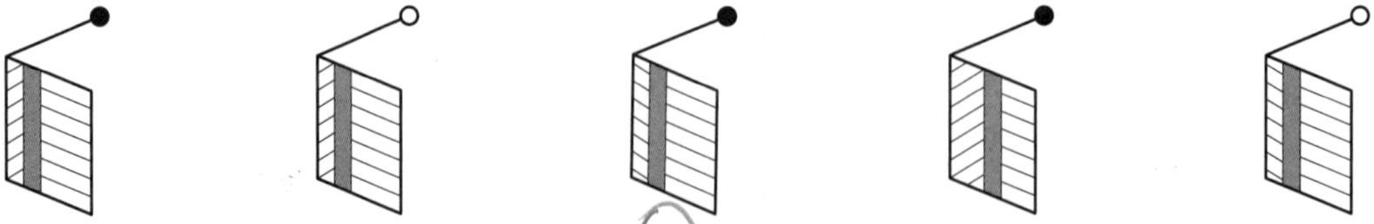

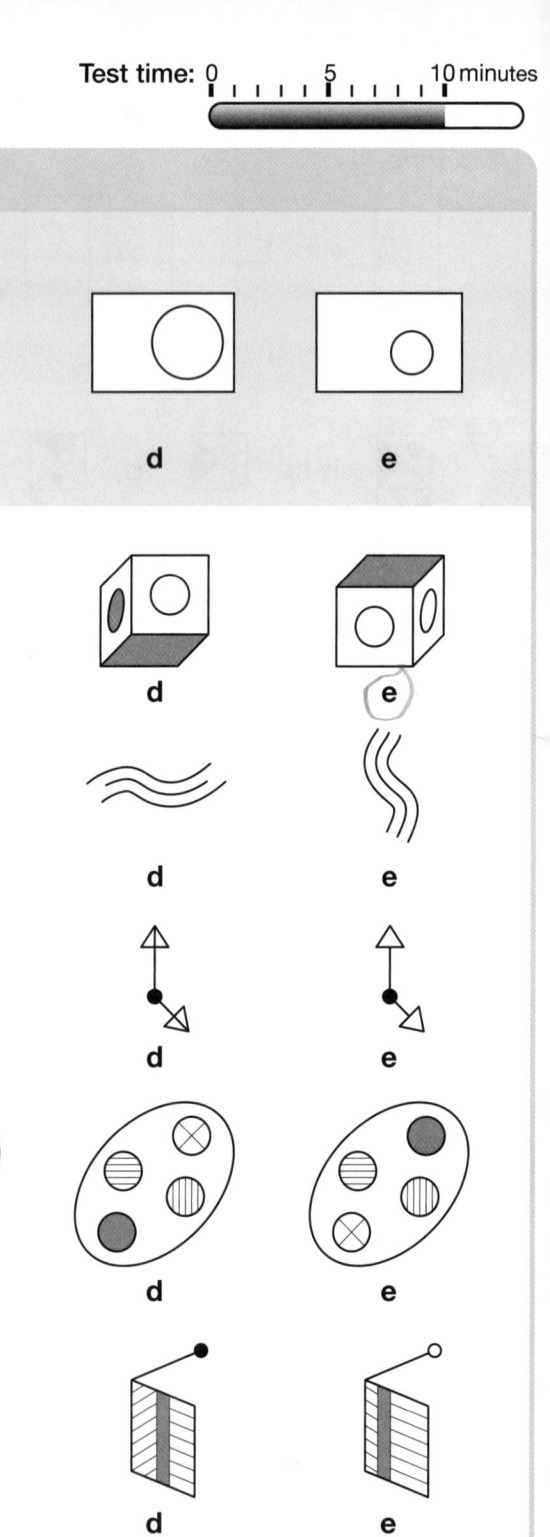

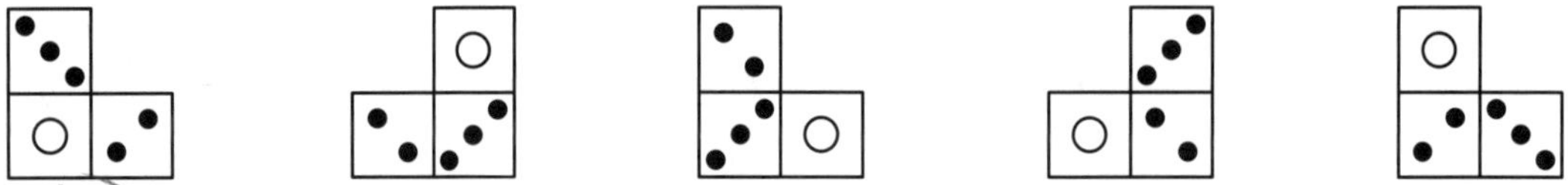

Which shape or pattern completes the second pair in the same way as the first pair?

**Example**

7
8
9
10
11
12

Time for a break! Go to Puzzle Page 42

# TEST 5: **Missing Shapes**

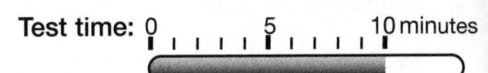

Test time: 0 5 10 minutes

Which one comes next?

***Example***

a b c (d) e

1

a b c d e

2

a b c d e

3

a b c d e

4

a b c d e

5

a b c d e

6

a b c d e

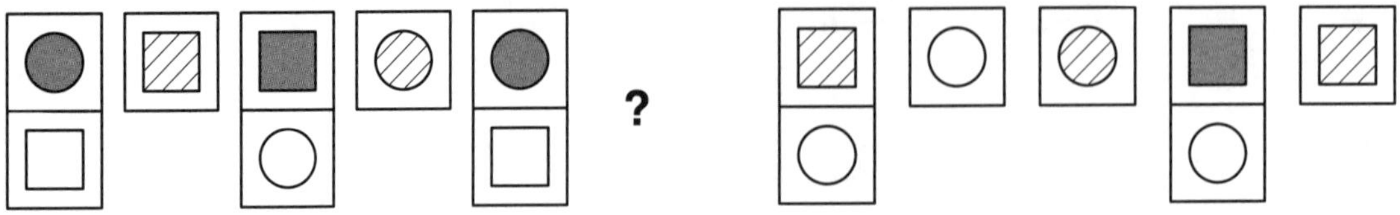

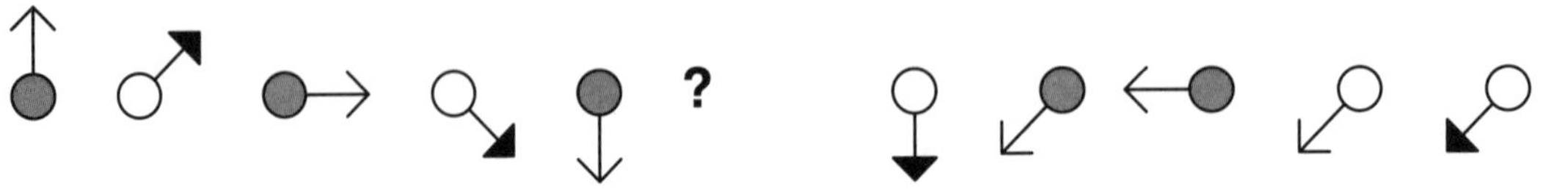

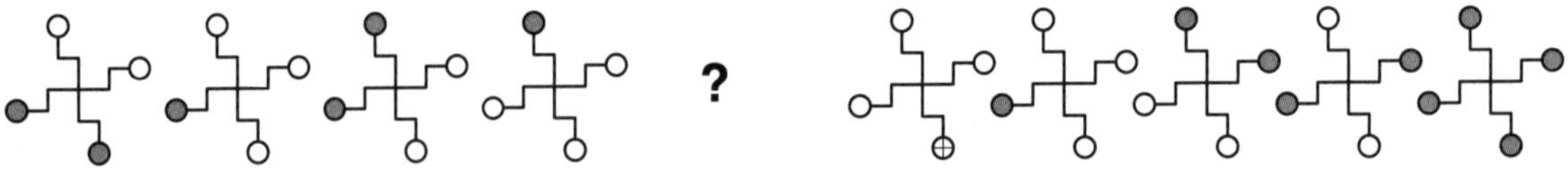

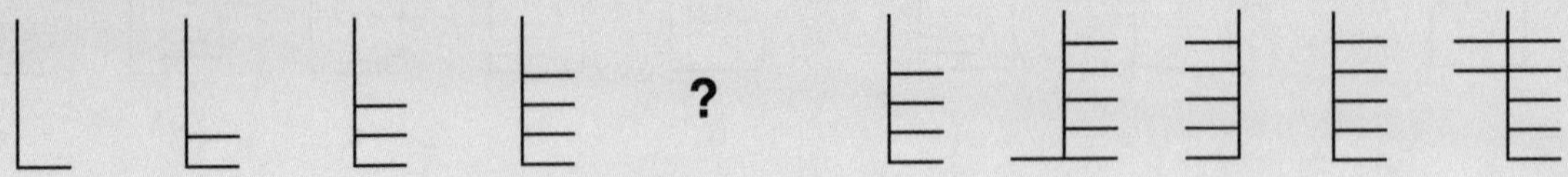

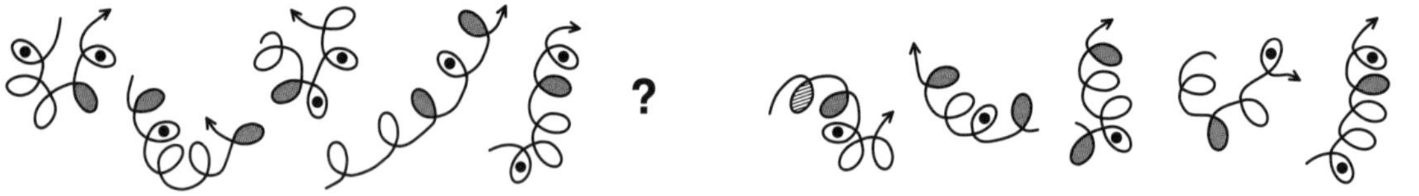

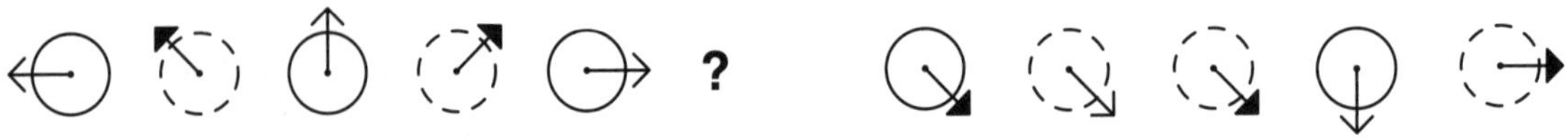

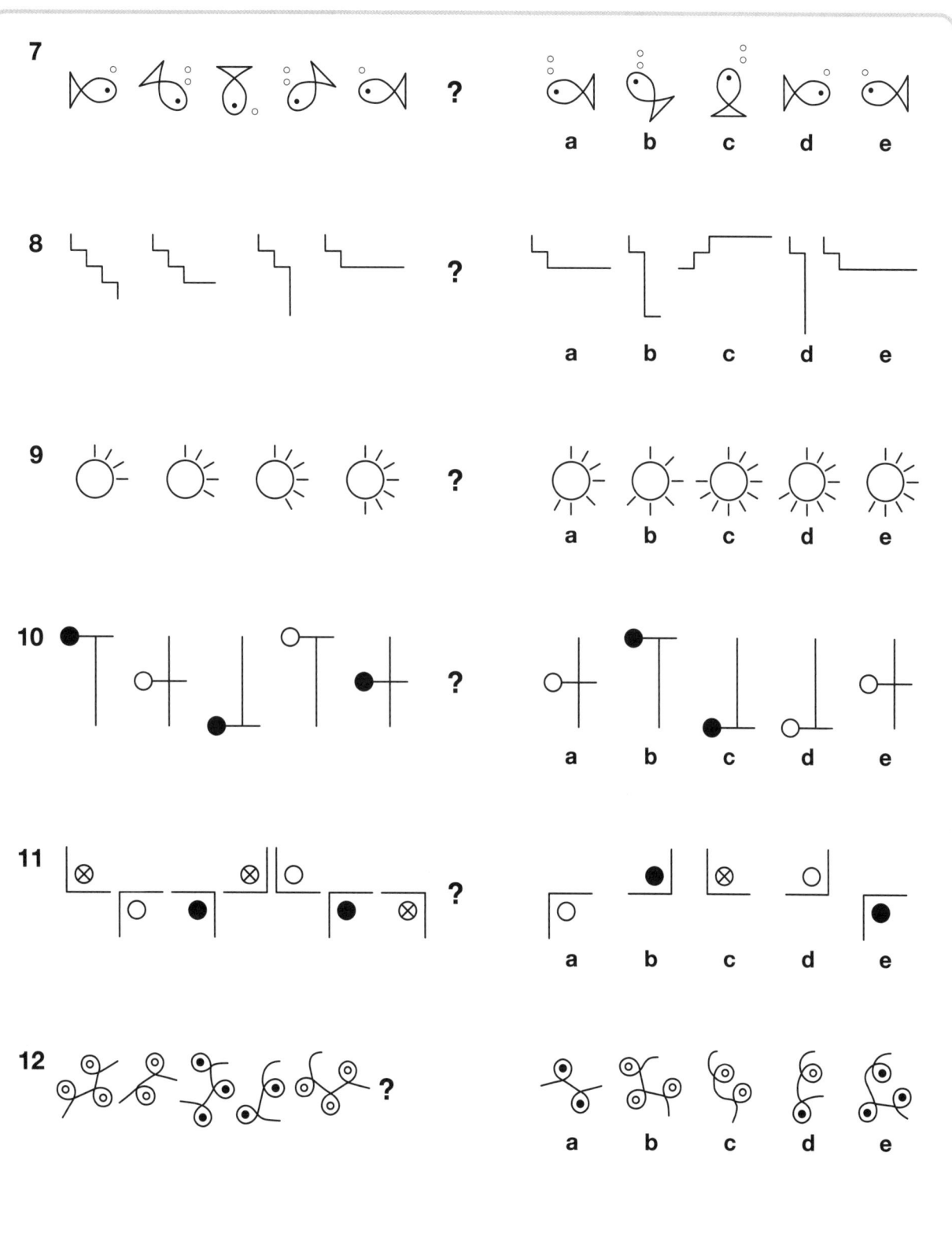

# TEST 6: **Identifying Shapes**

Test time: 0 5 10 minutes

Which is the odd one out?

***Example***

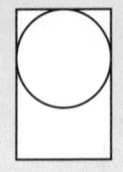

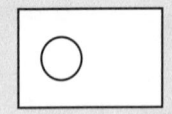

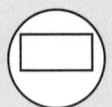

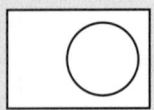

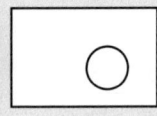

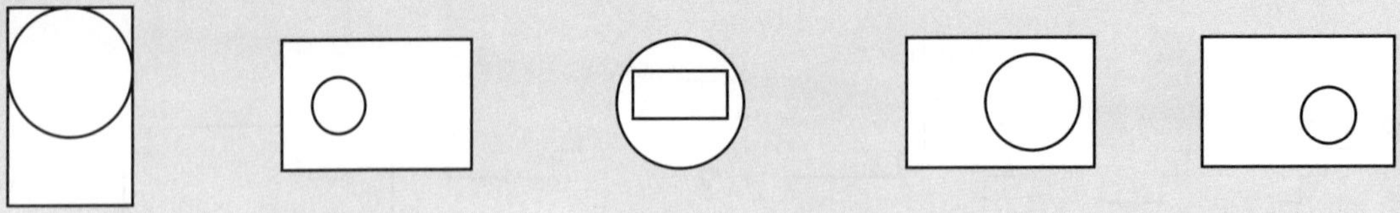

a b (c) d e

**1**

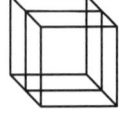

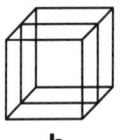

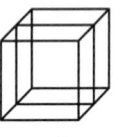

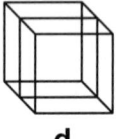

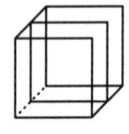

a b c d e

**2**

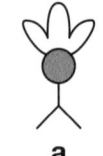

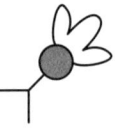

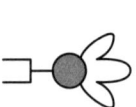

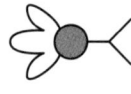

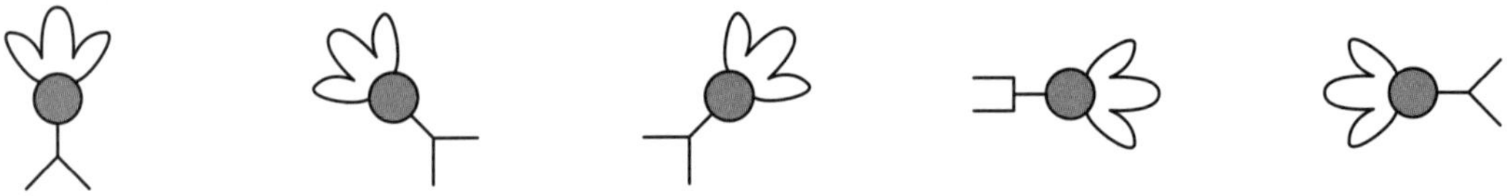

a b c d e

**3**

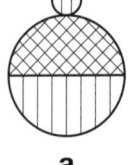

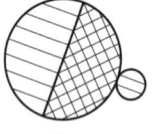

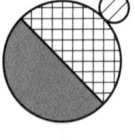

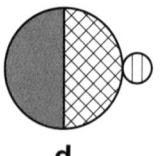

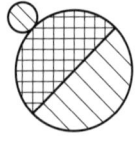

a b c d e

**4**

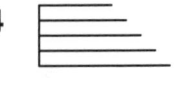

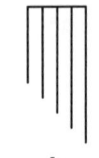

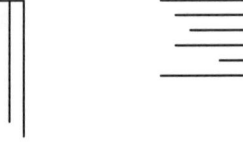

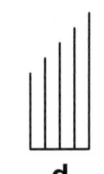

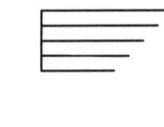

a b c d e

**5**

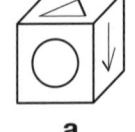

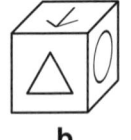

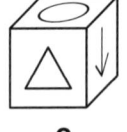

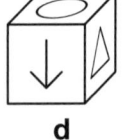

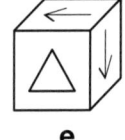

a b c d e

**6**

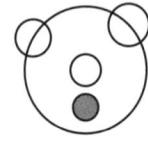

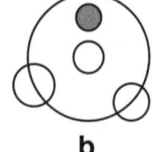

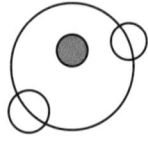

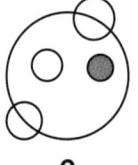

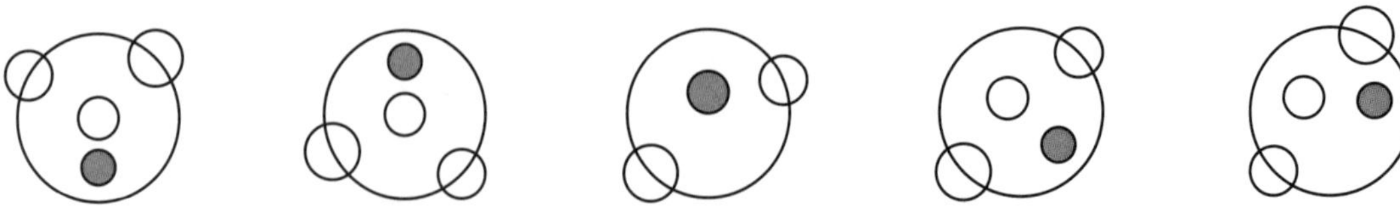

a b c d e

Which shape or pattern completes the second pair in the same way as the first pair?

*Example*

# Test 7: Missing Shapes

Test time: 0 — 5 — 10 minutes

**Which one comes next?**

*Example*

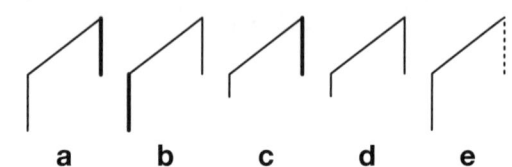

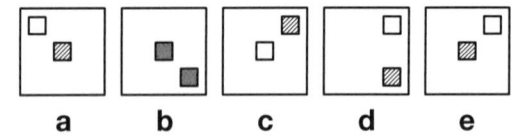

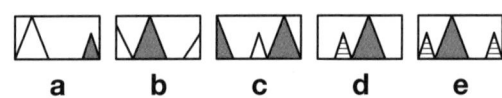

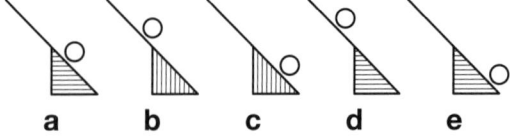

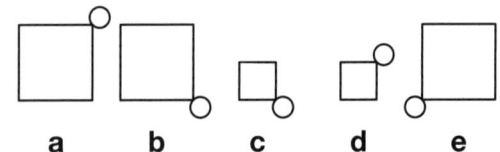

**Which shape or pattern completes the larger grid?**

*Example*

# Test 8: Rotating Shapes

Test time: 0 – 5 – 10 minutes

Which shape on the right is the reflection of the shape given on the left?

*Example*

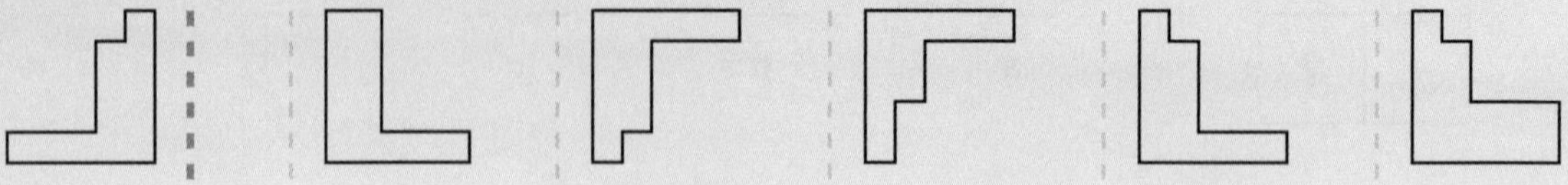

a  b  c  (d)  e

1 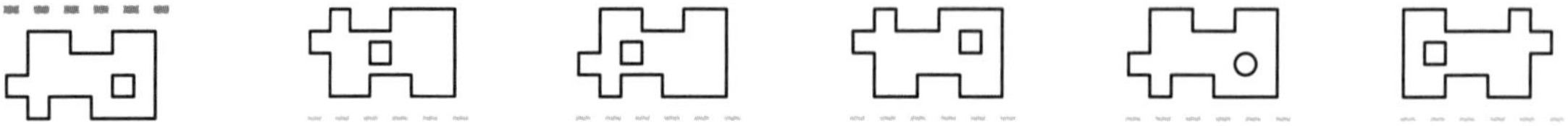
a  b  c  d  e

2
a  b  c  d  e

3
a  b  c  d  e

4 
a  b  c  d  e

5 
a  b  c  d  e

6
a  b  c  d  e

Which cube cannot be made from the given net?

*Example*

| | a | b | c | **d** | e |

| 7 | a | b | c | d | e |
| 8 | a | b | c | d | e |
| 9 | a | b | c | d | e |
| 10 | a | b | c | d | e |

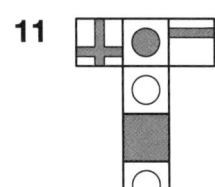 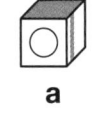  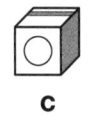 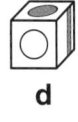 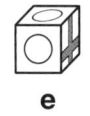

a　　b　　c　　d　　e

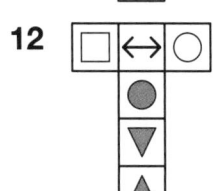 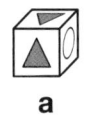 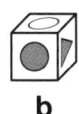   

a　　b　　c　　d　　e

*Time for a break! Go to Puzzle Page 43*

# Test 9: Missing Shapes

Which shape or pattern completes the larger grid?

*Example*

Which one comes next?

**Example**

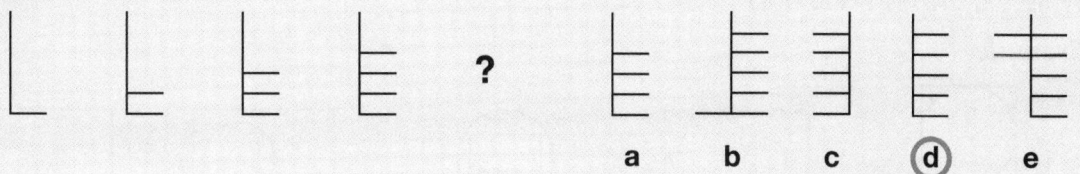

7 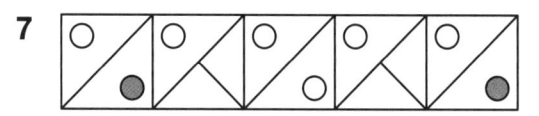 ?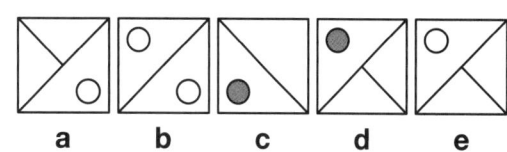

8 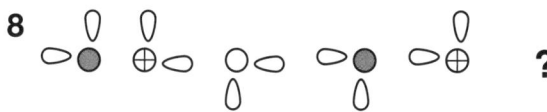 ?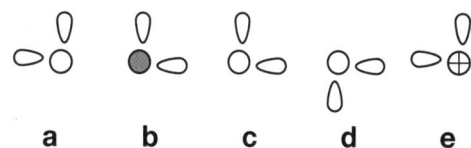

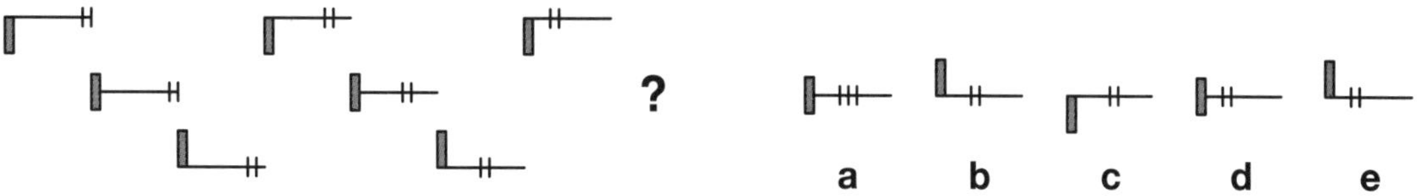

9 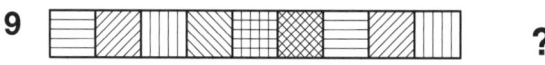 ?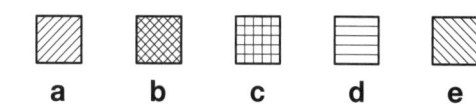

10 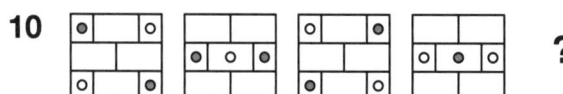 ?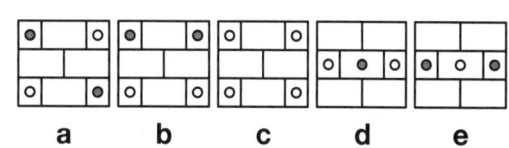

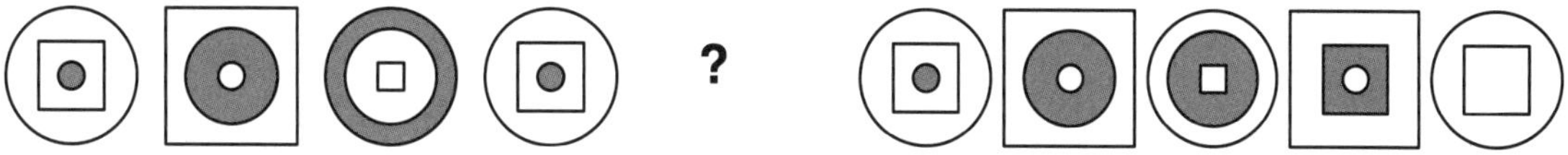

11

12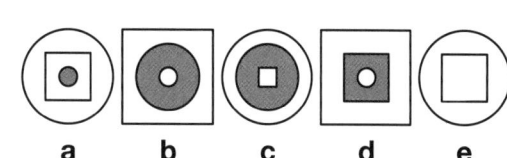

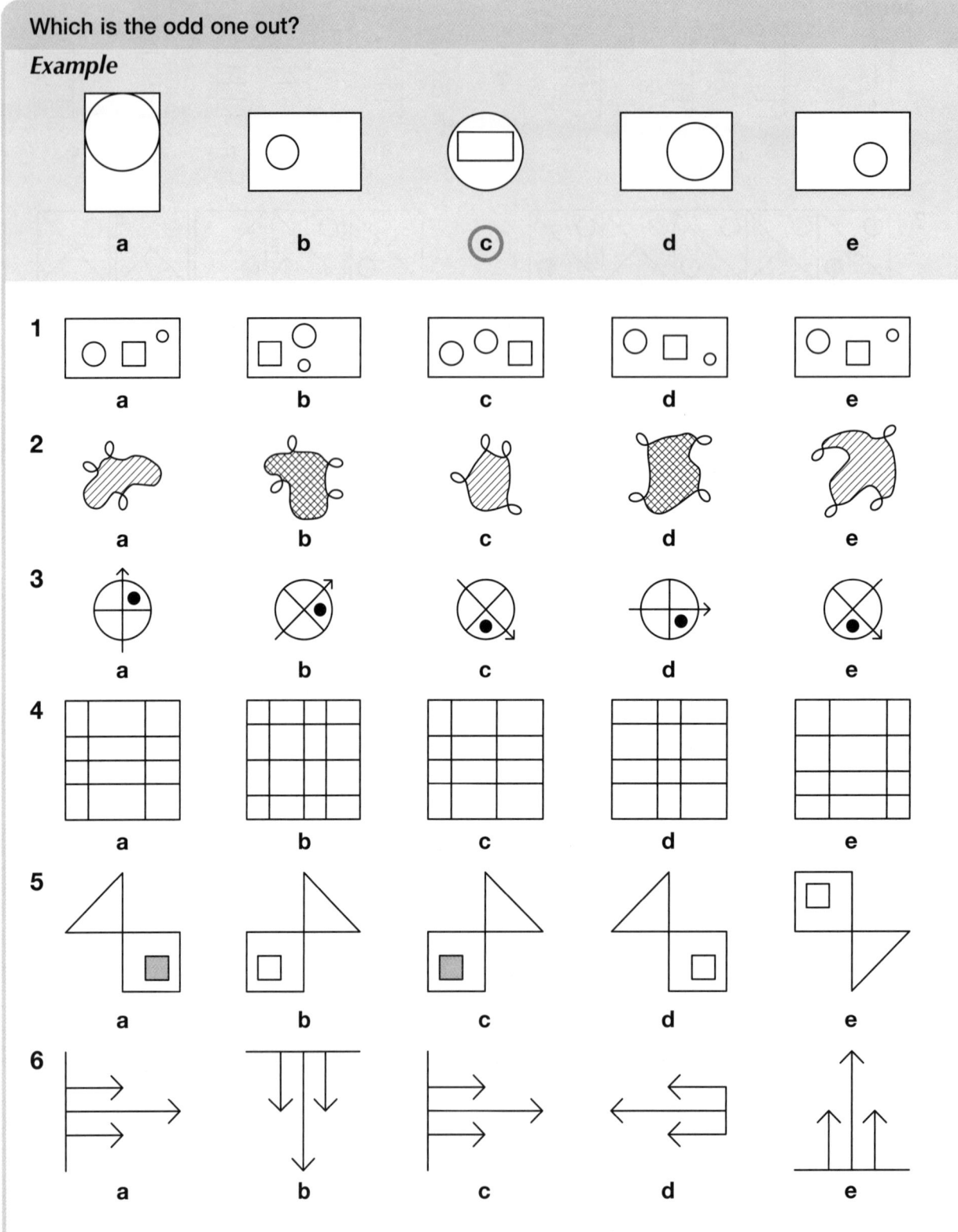

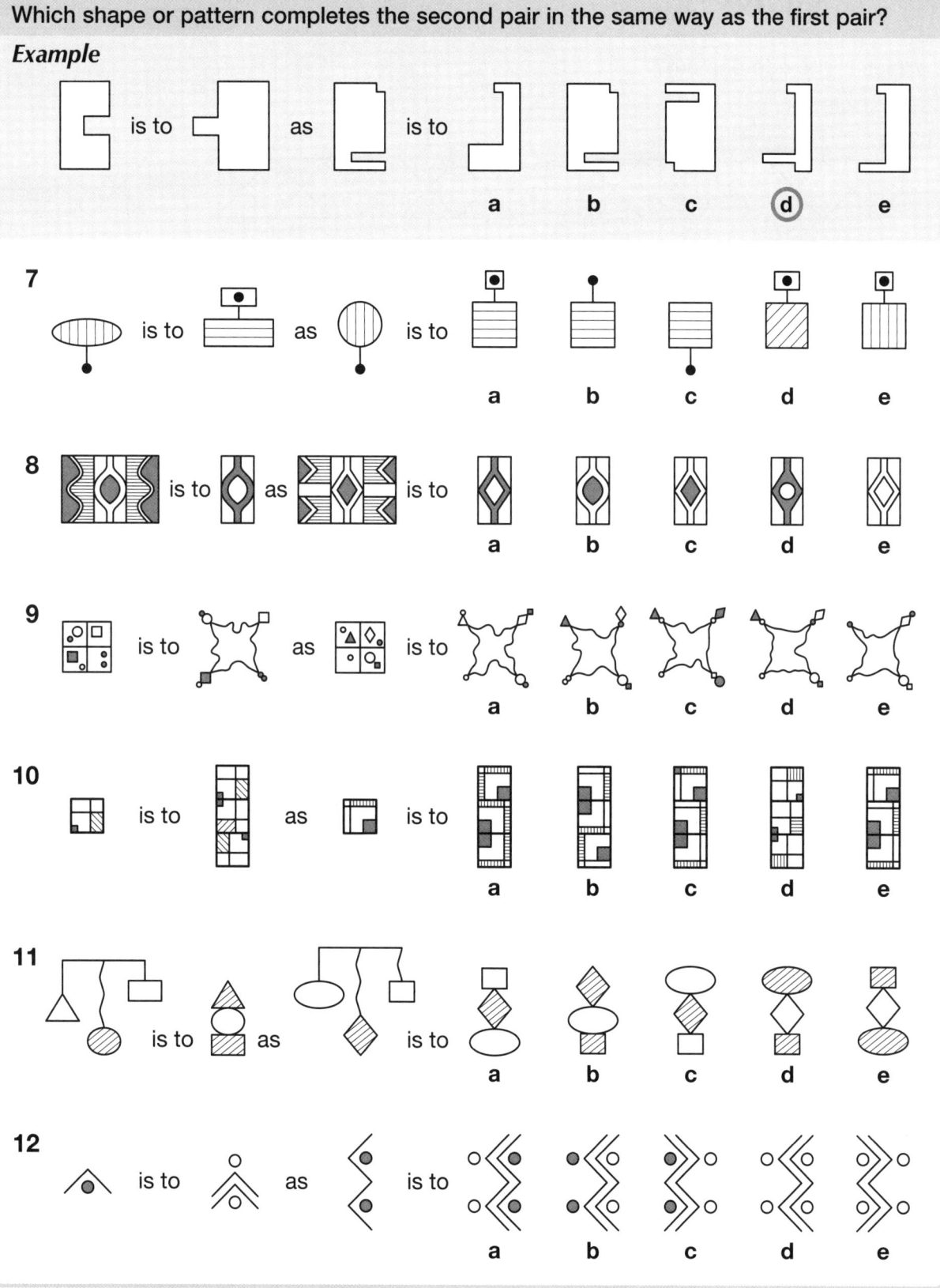

# Test 11: **Mixed**

Test time: 0 5 10 minutes

## Which is the odd one out?

**1**

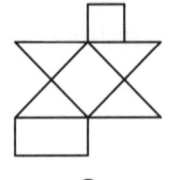

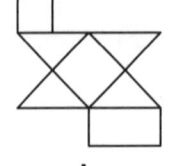

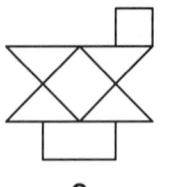

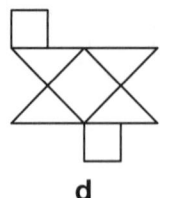

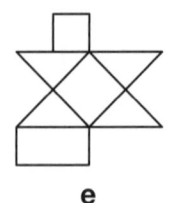

a b c d e

**2**

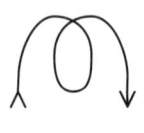

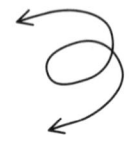

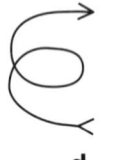

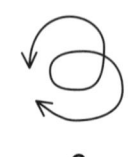

a b c d e

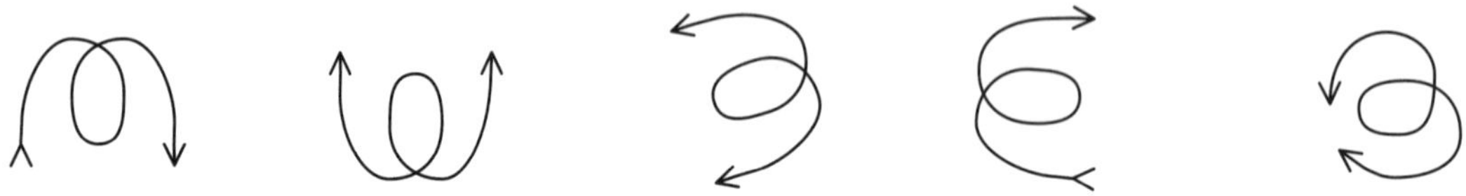

**3**

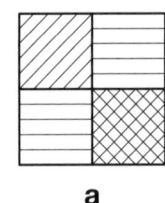

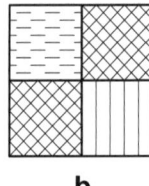

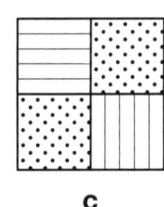

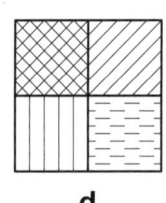

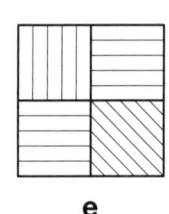

a b c d e

## Which shape or pattern completes the second pair in the same way as the first pair?

**4**

is to
as
is to
a
b
c
d
e

**5**

is to
as
is to
a
b
c
d
e

**6**

is to
as
is to
a
b
c
d
e

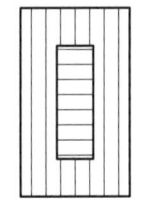

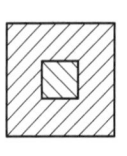

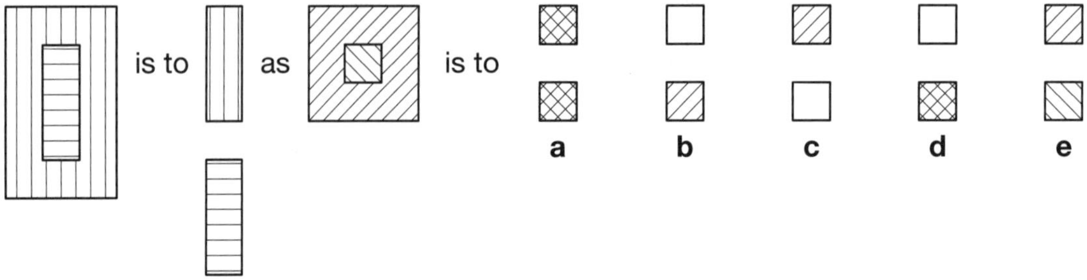

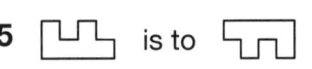

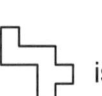

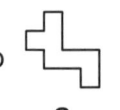

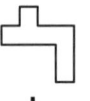

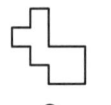

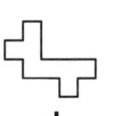

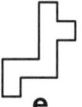

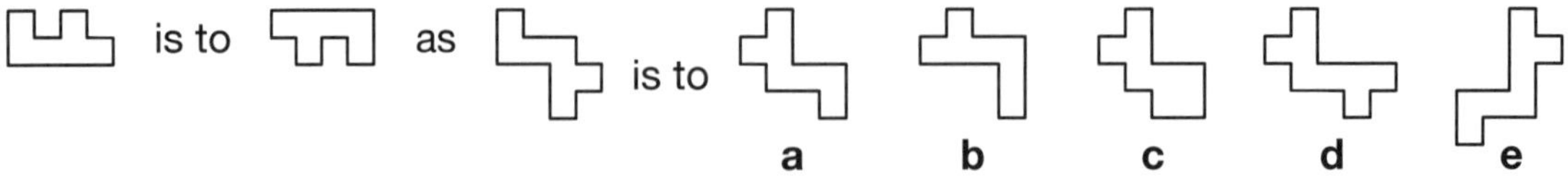

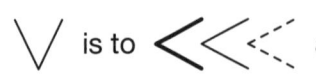

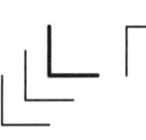

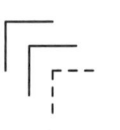

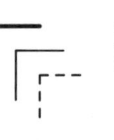

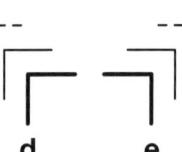

## In which larger shape is the shape on the left hidden?

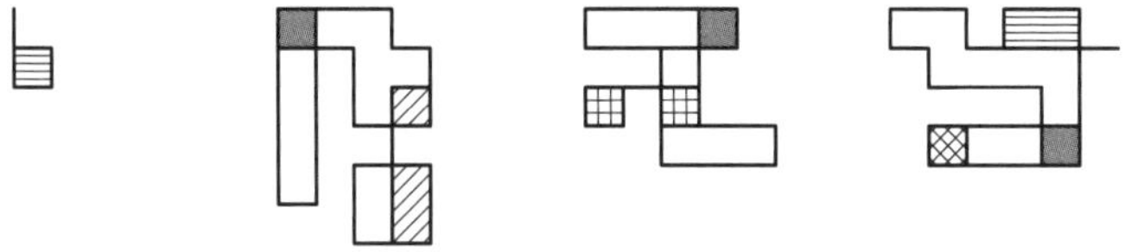

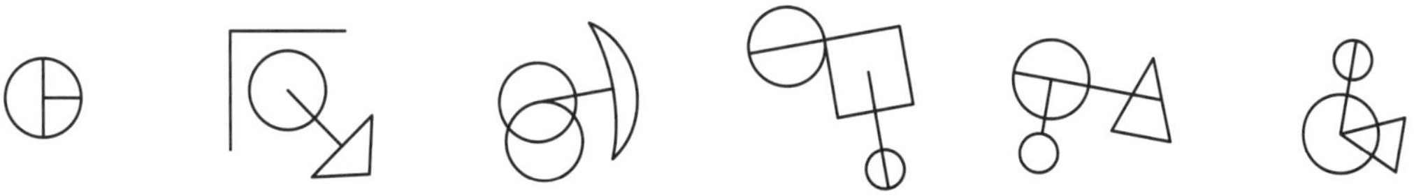

***Example***

a b c **d** e

**7**

a b c d e

**8**

a b c d e

**9**

a b c d e

## Which cube cannot be made from the given net?

**10**

a b c d e

**11**

a b c d e

**12**

a b c d e

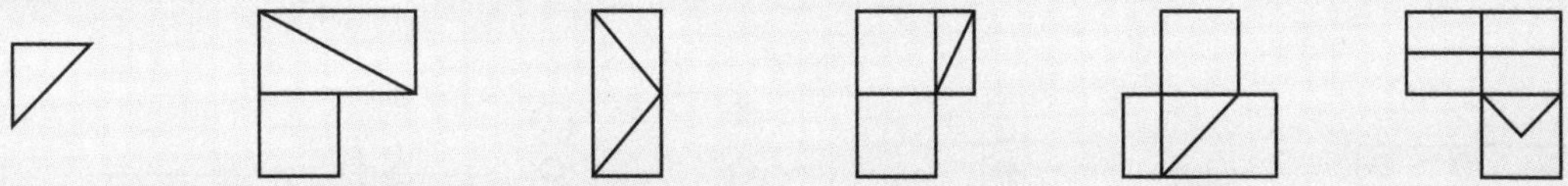

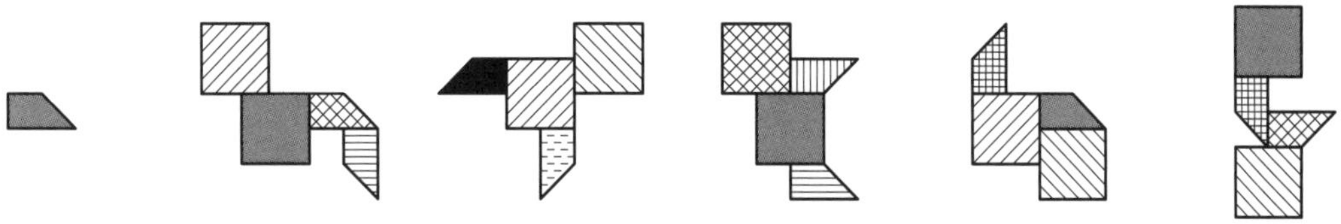

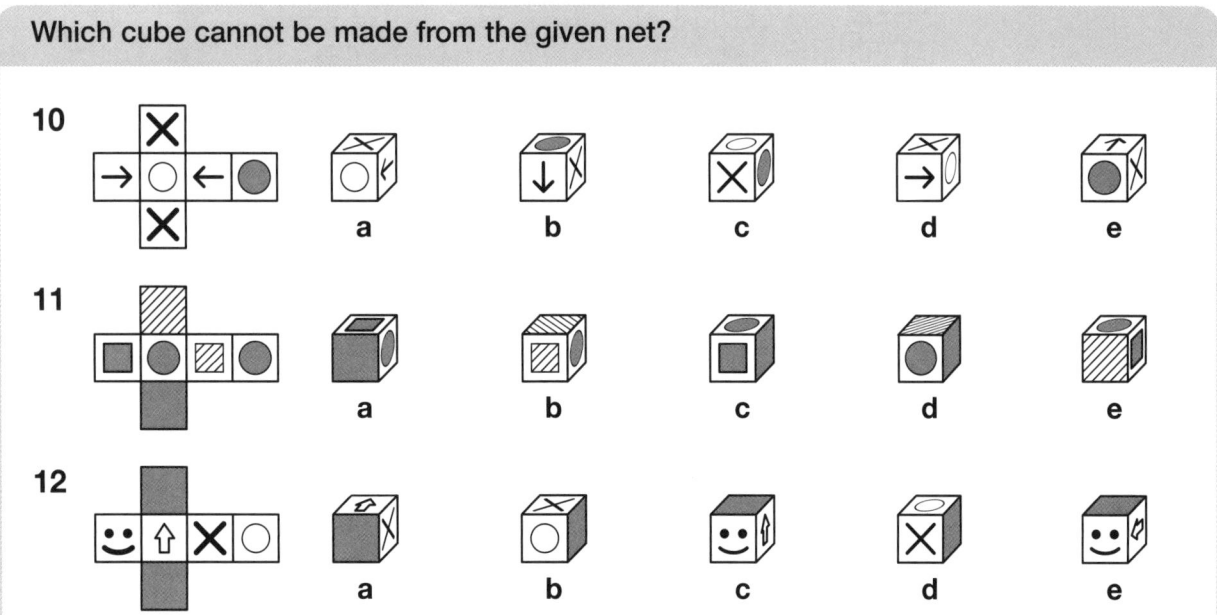

# TEST 12: **Mixed**

Test time: 0 5 10 minutes

**Which shape or pattern completes the second pair in the same way as the first pair?**

**1**

**2**

**3**

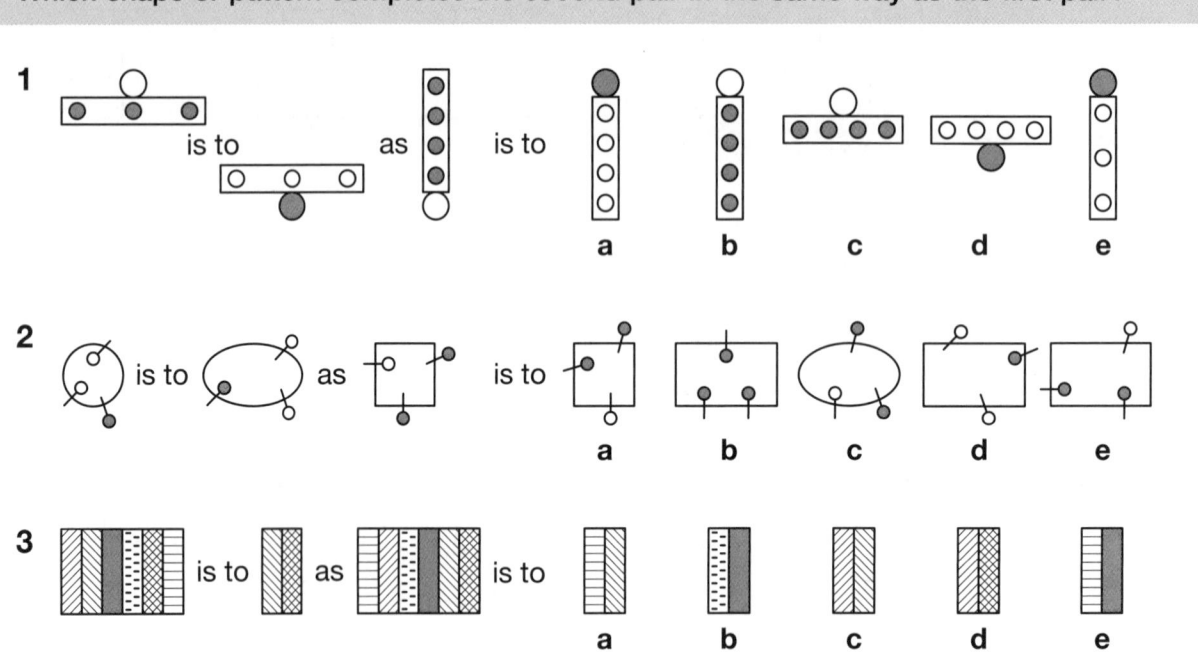

**In which larger shape is the shape on the left hidden?**

**4**

**5**

**6**

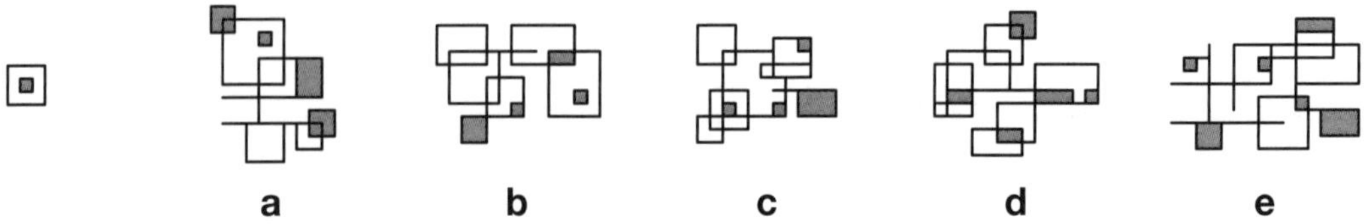

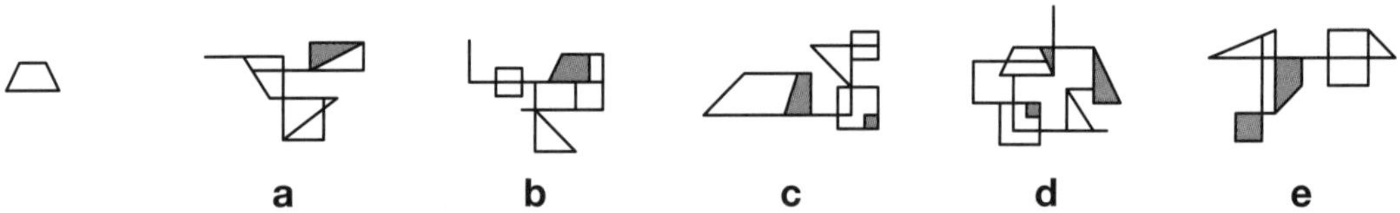

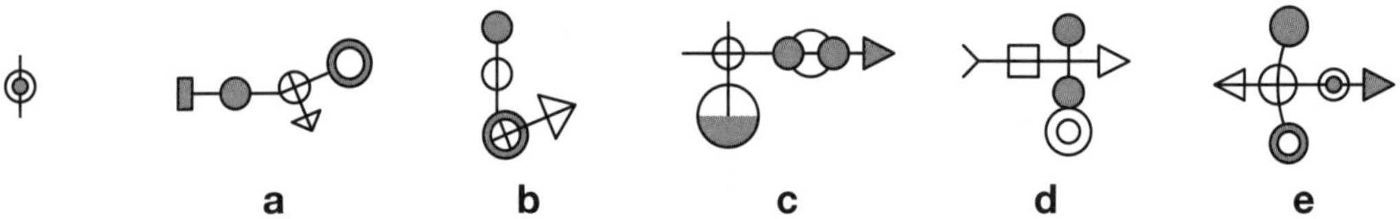

## Test 1 (pages 2–3)

1. **c** All of the other shapes have two continuous curved lines.
2. **e** All of the other shapes have one L-shaped line.
3. **d** All of the other shapes have two white circles and one black circle.
4. **e** All of the other shapes have one loop on the curly line.
5. **c** All of the other shapes have a vertical line dividing the circle.
6. **b** All of the other shapes have the white circle and arrow diagonally opposite.
7. **d** The given pattern is in top left and bottom right corner of the grid with the same pattern rotated 90° in the top right and bottom left.
8. **e** In the grid diagonally opposite squares are reflected; e is the mirror image of the top left square.

9. **c** The thick black arrow goes to white, the white circle stays and a black circle is added beside the white one.
10. **e** The whole shape is turned through 180° degrees; the white border of the triangle goes black and black centre goes white.
11. **c** None of the other shapes will fit into the spaces cut out of the given shape.

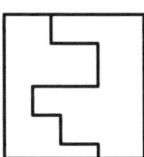

12. **e** Only e is a mirror image of the given shape with black and white shading reversed.

## Test 2 (pages 4–5)

1. **d** The first letter represents the direction of the line (A to the left, B up, C to the right, D down); the second letter represents the shading pattern of the circle (X is white, Y is grey, Z is a cross).
2. **c** The first letter represents the shape (L is a square, M a rectangle, N a triangle); the second letter represents the shading style (D is white, E is dots, F is cross-hatched, N is grey).
3. **e** The first letter represents the number of small white circles (A is 2, B is 3, C is 4); the second letter represents the number of small black circles (X is 2, Y is 3, Z is 4).
4. **d** The first letter represents the number of black spots in the shape (A is 3, B is 4, C is 5, D is 6); the second letter represents the numbers of crosses (X is 1, Y is 2, W is 3, Z is 4).
5. **e** The first letter represents the small shape at the top of each line (J is black circle, K is white circle, L is outline arrowhead, M is solid arrowhead); the second letter represents the small shape at the bottom (P is straight line, Q is white circle, R is solid black arrowhead, S is black circle).
6. **c** The first letter represents the number of short horizontal lines crossing the pattern (F is 1, E is 2, D is 3, G is 4); the second letter represents the number of lines in the 'steps' (R is 5, Q is 6, P is 7).
7. **d** The first letter represents the shading pattern in the circle (A is white, B is a cross, C is grey); the second letter represents the direction of the line from the large circle (P is up, R is down, S is to the left, Q is to the right).
8. **c** The first letter represents the shading style of the circle (D is white, E is a cross, F is black); the second letter represents the way that the square shape has been divided (A is in half, B a bar at the bottom, C a bar at the top).
9. **c** The first letter represents the style of shading in the shaded part of each pattern (X is vertical lines, Y is diagonal lines, Z is grey); the second letter represents the number of white circles in the pattern (A is 1, B is 2, C is 3).
10. **e** The first letter represents the size and shape of each pattern (A is small square, B is small circle, C is large circle, D is large square); the second letter represents the style of shading (R is horizontal lines, S is vertical lines, T is cross-hatched lines).
11. **d** The first letter represents the line style at the end of each curved line (A is simple arrowhead, B is short straight line, C is inverted V); the second letter represents the shading of the circles along the curved line (X is black, Y is a cross, Z is white).

12 **b** The first letter represents the orientation of the central black and white circle (D is top half black, E is lower half black, F is right side black); the second letter represents the number of small white circles in the shape (A is 5, B is 4, C is 3).

## Test 3 (pages 6–7)

1. **d** All of the other shapes have a white square; d has a white rectangle.
2. **d** All of the other shapes have a V-shape at the end of the curved arrow.
3. **b** All of the other shapes have lines of equal length in both the top and bottom of the double-lined step element.
4. **a** All of the other shapes are straight cylinders.
5. **e** All of the other shapes have the middle black circle off centre and touching the surrounding circle line.
6. **d** All of the other shapes have two triangles in the top section of the pattern.
7. **c** The second half of the pair is a repeat of the third square from the column of four squares.
8. **b** The number of triangles gives the number of circles; the circle shading is the same as in the lower part of the triangles.
9. **d** The number of small shapes gives the number of lines in the zigzag, with the same small shape at each end.
10. **a** The top shape decreases to fit inside the middle shape, which also decreases in size to fit inside the bottom shape, and the whole is then located in a white square. The shading patterns do not change.
11. **e** The number of 'loops' along the given curved line gives the number of circles and the loop shading from left to right is copied in the circles from top to bottom.
12. **c** The second half of the pattern is one quarter of the given shape.

## Test 4 (pages 8–9)

1. **e** All of the other shapes show two adjacent faces with one white circle and one grey circle.
2. **d** All of the other shapes have three lines of equal length.
3. **c** All of the other shapes have the same style of arrowhead on both lines.
4. **b** All of the circles in each set, apart from those in b, have different styles of shading.
5. **d** All of the other shapes have the grey vertical line off centre.
6. **a** All of the other shapes have the square with three black dots adjacent to the square with two back dots.
7. **e** The central square becomes a circle with opposite diagonal shading; the white circles given on the outside change to black and the black ones to white.
8. **e** The shape is turned 90° clockwise, the black section becomes white and two small lines in opposite directions are added to the top.
9. **c** The middle black shape changes to white and there is one at the top and one at the bottom of the pattern; the white outer shape changes to black and sits in the middle of the pattern.
10. **b** The whole shape turns 90° anti-clockwise, white circles stay white, the black circle changes to have diagonal line shading, and the + and – lines stay in the same position.
11. **e** From left to right in the given pattern, the lines indicate the number of shapes, the middle element gives the shape and the third part gives the shading style.
12. **e** The irregular shapes become a circle in a square, with the black dots moving into the square and the crosses into the circle. The number of dots and crosses is unchanged.

## Test 5 (pages 10–11)

1. **e** Double and single squares alternate; the shapes in the double squares alternate from top to bottom with the shape at the bottom being the shape in the next single square; the shading style is the same in all of the double squares and all of the single squares.
2. **e** The style of the arrowhead and circle shading alternate along the sequence, with the arrow turning 45° clockwise each time.
3. **c** Two black circles alternate with one black circle, the position of the black circles moves round clockwise 90° each time.
4. **e** The pattern increases with an extra line each time; the arrowhead style and small line/shape at the opposite end of the pattern alternate.
5. **c** The position of the shaded loops along the curved line form a repeating sequence of four patterns, so the next pattern will be the same as the second one in the series.
6. **c** The circle line style and the arrow head style alternate and the arrow rotates 45° clockwise each time.
7. **b** The 'fish' shape rotates 45° clockwise each time and the number of 'bubbles' alternates.
8. **d** The number of lines in the step pattern reduces by one each time, with the end line increasing in length each time.
9. **e** The number of lines around the circle increases by one each time.

10 **d** The pin shape moves from top to middle to bottom then back to the top, the circle shading alternates between black and white.
11 **d** The L-shape turns 90° clockwise each time, the circle shading pattern sequence is cross, white, black, cross, etc.
12 **c** The number of loops alternates between two and three, the shading pattern for the small circles is: after the first shape there are two shapes with white circle, then two shapes with black circle, etc.

## Test 6 (pages 12–13)

1 **e** All of the other shapes have solid lines along each edge of the cuboids.
2 **d** All of the other shapes have an inverted V at the base of the straight line.
3 **d** All of the other shapes have the same shading in the small circle.
4 **c** All of the other shapes have five parallel lines.
5 **e** All of the other shapes have faces showing an arrow, a circle and a triangle.
6 **c** All of the other shapes have a black circle and a small white circle inside the larger circle.
7 **d** The shaded rectangle becomes white with a narrow shaded rectangle on one side and a thin line on the other side.
8 **c** The four small shapes become shaded grey and move to the outside of the larger shape; the dividing crossing lines become wide white bands.
9 **a** The pattern is rotated through 90° clockwise.
10 **d** The shape becomes shaded and projects into a white square from the right hand side of the square.
11 **e** The spot on the arrow goes from white to black; it has a shorter similar arrow on the left and a longer similar arrow on the right.
12 **a** The inner shape becomes the outer shape and the outer shape becomes the inner shape.

## Test 7 (pages 14–15)

1 **c** The lower left line alternates between long and short; the higher right side line alternates in style between thin, dotted and thick lines.
2 **e** One small white square rotates clockwise around the corners of the larger white square; the shading of the small square in the centre is in the sequence dark grey, white, diagonal shading.
3 **d** The vertical arrows have one white circle and alternate between pointing up and pointing down; these vertical arrows alternate with a horizontal pattern which has an increasing number of circles each time.
4 **d** The pattern moves along the bottom of the rectangle; the pattern is made up of a large grey triangle with a small white one next to it, then a space and another large grey triangle with a small striped triangle next to it, then a space before the pattern is repeated.
5 **e** The white circle moves down the sloping line each time and the shading of the triangle alternates between horizontal and vertical lines.
6 **b** The white circle rotates clockwise around the corners of the square at each step and the squares form a sequence: from large to middle-sized to small to large, etc.
7 **e** The missing square is a mirror image of the top left square, with the line of reflection going from top right to bottom left of the grid.

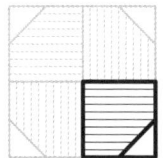

8 **b** Diagonally opposite patterns are similar, the missing piece is the same as the top left section rotated through 180°.

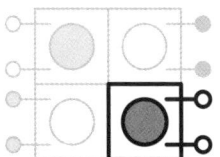

9 **d** A short diagonal line from the top left corner completes the X pattern; the shaded rectangle rotates 90° around the grid.

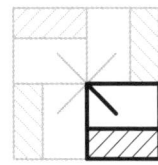

10 **e** Both sides of each line have the same shape, with the left side being white and large and the right side being black and small; the short lines outside of the grid on the left are reflected on the right side.

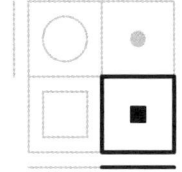

11 **d** Both the L-shaped line inside the square the L-shape on the outer corners rotate 90° clockwise around the grid.

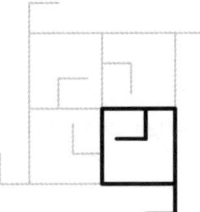

12 **e** The pattern in each square of the grid is reflected both vertically and horizontally with the shading switching from white to black and black to white.

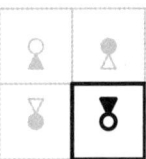

## Test 8 (pages 16–17)

*Questions 1–6: To check and understand the answers for questions asking for reflections, use a small mirror held vertically along the dotted line so that the pattern is reflected in the mirror. This allows the pattern that is the exact reflection of the given shape to be observed.*

1 **c**
2 **e**
3 **d**
4 **d**
5 **b**

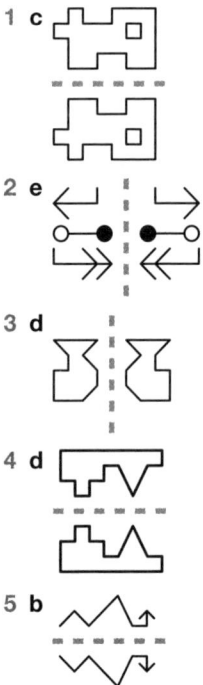

6 **e**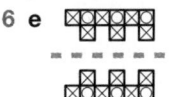

7 **b** The grey square will share an edge with the base edge of the black 'flame' shape and the white 'flame' shape, so cannot be adjacent to it as shown in option b.

8 **b** The grey triangle points towards the grey circle, so the net cannot form cube b.

9 **e** The face with the white circle and grey surround cannot be adjacent to the face with the grey circle and white surround, so the net cannot form cube e.

10 **d** The face with the white circle cannot be adjacent to the face with the three black spots so the net cannot form cube d.

11 **e** The two faces with white circles are not adjacent in the net, they will be opposite in the cube and cannot form cube e.

12 **c** The face with the white square will be opposite the face with the white circle, so the net cannot form cube c.

## Test 9 (pages 18–19)

1 **e** The missing pattern is a reflection of the top left quarter of the grid, when the line of reflection is placed diagonally from top right to bottom left.

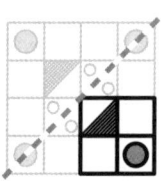

2 **c** The small square and circle in the missing part are a reflection of the top left quarter; the short straight line rotates 90° moving round the grid.

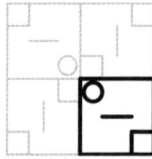

3 **c** The missing pattern is the same as the pattern in the top left quarter; lower left and top right are the same.

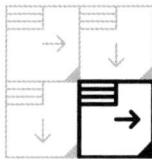

4 **d** The arrow points from top left to the centre to complete the pattern in the middle of the grid; the pattern on the outer part of the squares rotates 90° round the whole grid.

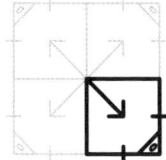

5 **c** The pattern in all of the squares within the grid is the same.
6 **e** The lower squares in the grid are a reflection of the upper squares with a horizontal mirror line; the outline of the white shapes is dotted in the lower squares.

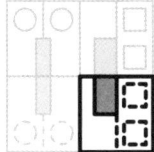

7 **e** The top left triangle in each square is the same; the lower right triangle alternates between black circle and short line.
8 **c** The two 'petal' shapes rotate clockwise 90° along the sequence; the pattern of the central circle follows a sequence of grey–cross–white–black–etc.
9 **e** The sequence of the shading pattern in the squares is horizontal lines, diagonal lines (bottom left to top right), vertical lines, diagonal lines (top left to bottom right) squared grid, diagonal grid; this sequence is then repeated.
10 **a** The first and third patterns are the same and the second and fourth patterns are the same; the fifth pattern will be the same as the first and third.
11 **d** The horizontal line moves down the solid rectangle, then reverts back to the top; the two short vertical lines are in the same relative position for three patterns then move closer to the black rectangle for the next three patterns.
12 **b** The large outer shape becomes the central shape in the next pattern with the other two shapes increasing in size; the shading is unchanged. The fifth shape will be the same as the second.

## Test 10 (pages 20–21)

1 **c** All of the other shapes have a small circle and a larger circle.
2 **a** All of the other shapes have four 'loops' on the outside of the shape.
3 **e** All of the other shapes have both ends of the arrow extending outside the circle.
4 **b** All of the other shapes have three columns.
5 **e** All of the other shapes have the square element of the pattern below the triangle.
6 **d** All of the other shapes have the arrows projecting from a line which extends beyond the junctions with the three arrows.
7 **a** The circle changes to a square, the vertical shading to horizontal shading and the black spot is within a small square above the larger square.
8 **a** The pattern is reduced to the central third element, with the white and dark shading reversed.
9 **d** The shapes in each quarter of the grid join on the outside of an irregular shape, in the same relative positions around the shape.
10 **e** The shape is repeated at the top of a column and then rotated through 90° for the middle section and rotated again for the lowest square; the shading does not change.
11 **d** The three shapes are placed in a column, with the left one at the top; diagonal shading becomes white and white becomes diagonal shading.
12 **d** The zig zag line is doubled and circles are repeated on both sides with shading changed from grey to white.

## Test 11 (pages 22–23)

1 **d** All of the other shapes have a rectangle at the bottom of the pattern.
2 **e** All of the other shapes have identical 'loops' in the patterns.
3 **d** All of the other shapes have two opposite squares with the same shading.
4 **e** The shape in the centre of the pattern is repeated twice, with the lower copy having the same shading as in the original and the upper one taking the shading of the large outer shape.
5 **a** The shape is rotated through 180°.
6 **c** The shape is rotated clockwise 90° and with a thick-line copy of the pattern to the left and a dotted line copy of the pattern to the right.
7 **e** None of the other shapes has a small square with horizontal line shading within them.

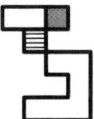

8  **d** None of the other shapes has a circle with a diameter line and with one of the semi-circles divided again by a radius to give quarters.

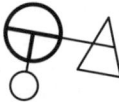

9  **d** Only shapes b and d have a grey shaded trapezium shape but the trapezium in b is a mirror image of the given shape.

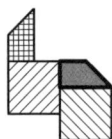

10  **c** The face with the white circle and the face with the grey circle must be opposite so they cannot be adjacent in the cube.
11  **d** The face with the solid grey shading and the face with the diagonal line shading must be opposite in the cube, not adjacent.
12  **e** The white arrow on one face points towards a solid grey-shaded face, so cannot point to the 'smiley' face.

### Test 12 (pages 24–25)

1  **a** The pattern is rotated through 180° and the shading of the circles is reversed.
2  **e** The shape is stretched (circle to oval; square to rectangle) and the orientation (pointing into or out of the shape) of the 'pins' is reversed.
3  **c** The pattern is reduced to just the second and fifth columns from the first rectangle.
4  **c** None of the other patterns has a small white square with a small grey square in its centre.

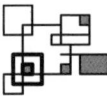

5  **d** All of the other shapes have shaded or irregular trapeziums.

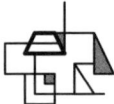

6  **e** None of the other shapes has a small white circle with a smaller grey circle within it and a line through it.

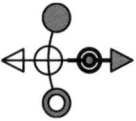

7  **e** The missing pattern is a reflection of the top left square, when reflected in a diagonal mirror line from bottom left to top right across the grid.

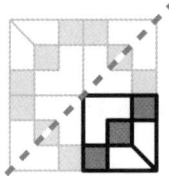

8  **d** The missing pattern is a reflection of the top left square, when reflected in a diagonal mirror line from bottom left to top right across the grid.

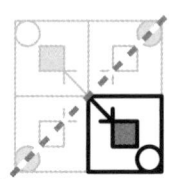

9  **e** The pattern in each square within the grid is rotated by 90° progressively around the grid.

10  **d**

11  **c**

12  **d**

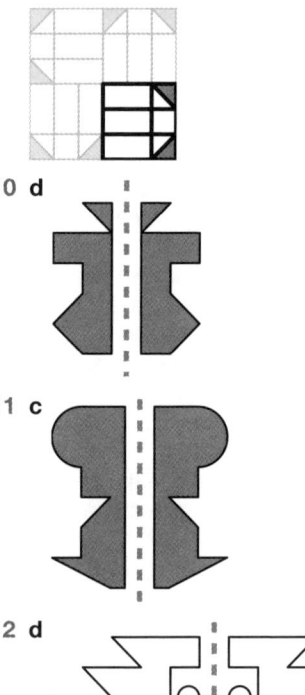
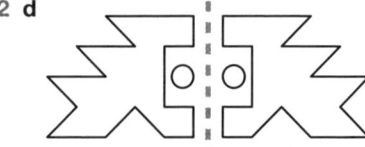

## Test 13 (pages 26–27)

1. **d** The number of small grey circles increases by one, the number of small white circles decreases by one and the number of short lines crossing the circumference alternates between three and one.
2. **e** The two vertical lines move progressively across the rectangle from left to right, the white circle and the circle with the X alternate and the small grey circle is always at the left end.
3. **d** The triangle rotates by 90° clockwise each time with the shading of the square following a repeated pattern of diagonal lines –white–black spot–etc.
4. **a** The pattern in the top left is repeated in the bottom right square of the grid.

5. **c** The bottom right square in the grid is a reflection of the pattern in the top left square, with a diagonal reflection line from the bottom left to the top right of the grid.

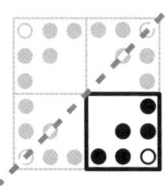

6. **b** The squares with the arrows rotate 90° around the grid; the central pattern has identical shapes diagonally opposite each other.

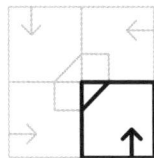

7. **e** The first letter represents the orientation of the patterned bar across the circle; the second letter represents the shading style in that bar.
8. **d** The first letter represents the number of grey circles in the pattern; the second letter represents the position of the short line projecting from the top of the grid.
9. **e** The first letter represents the style of the arrowhead; the second letter indicates the style of the arrow tail.

10. **c**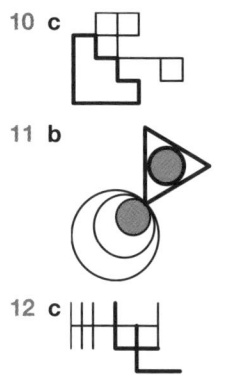

11. **b**

12. **c**

## Test 14 (pages 28–29)

1. **d** The black circle is on alternate shapes, alternating from left to right on the top line, the white circle in the middle alternates from a left to right position and the white circle at the bottom is on alternate shapes, alternating from left to right.
2. **e** The sequence of the shapes is circle–triangle (flat base)–rectangle–triangle (point at base)–etc, the central dot alternates from white to grey, the line from the centre rotates 45° clockwise and with a grey dot at the end of alternate lines.
3. **c** The horizontal bar in the first and then alternate shapes has a decreasing number of squares, with alternate squares shaded and a grey circle moves up its vertical bar, in the other shapes there are always two white squares in the horizontal bar and a grey square moves progressively up the vertical bar.
4. **d**
5. **e**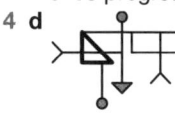
6. **a**
7. **e** (refer to Test 8 Q1–6 reflections)

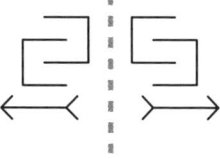

8 **b** (refer to test 8 Q1–6 reflections)

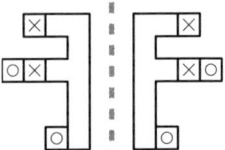

9 **d** (refer to test 8 Q1–6 reflections)

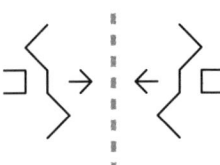

10 **e** The first letter represents the number of black spots on the square (D is 1, C is 2, B is 3 and A is 4); the second letter represents the position and orientation of the L-shape (K is on the bottom pointing right, J is on the bottom pointing left, L is on the right pointing down, M is on the right pointing up).

11 **d** The first letter represents the fraction of the 'flag' shaded (P is 1/3, Q is 1/2 and R is 2/3); the second letter represents the shape at the top of the 'flagpole' (C is a grey circle, B is a white circle, A is a white oval).

12 **c** The first letter represents the style of the mouth (L is a smile, M is a sad face, N is a straight line); the second letter represents the hair style (C is one curly hair, B is four strands, T is for two tufts).

## Test 15 (pages 30–31)

1 **e** The shape alternates along the sequence, with the number of short straight lines increasing by one every two shapes, and the lines crossing a horizontal top line have wider spacing than those crossing the vertical line when it is at the top of the shape. The main pattern of lines alternates between the two options so the next item must have be the same as the second and fourth in the sequence.

2 **b** The plain white octagons alternate with changing smaller shapes which all have an inner grey shape that becomes the outer shape for the next small shape.

3 **d** The x, the triangle and the circle move progressively through the grid in a zig-zag way: towards the right across the top, then down to the middle row and move left across it, then down to the bottom line and across to the right; after one blank square the pattern of shapes is repeated in reverse.

4 **d** The square to complete the grid is a reflection of the top left square, with the line of reflection diagonally from bottom left to top right.

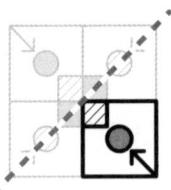

5 **e** The patterns in each square are identical, they are rotated 90° each move round the grid.

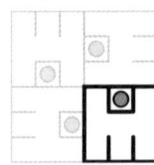

6 **a** The diagonal shading of the squares on the left is reflected in a vertical mirror line in the bars of the squares on the right; any vertical shading on the left becomes horizontal shading on the right and vice versa.

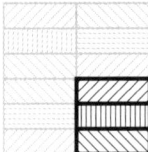

7 **b** (refer to Test 8 Q1–6 reflections)

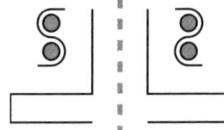

8 **d** (refer to Test 8 Q1–6 reflections)

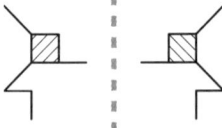

9 **d** (refer to Test 8 Q1–6 reflections)

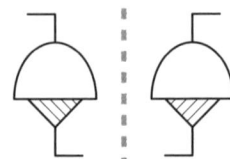

10 **c**

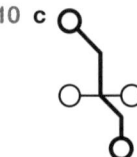

11 e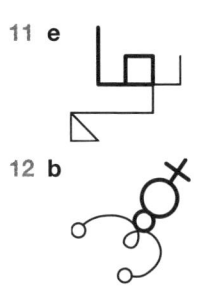

12 b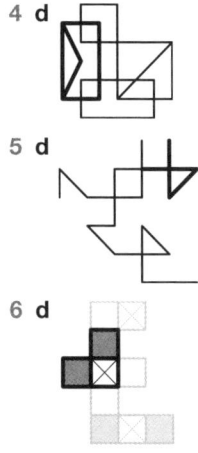

## Test 16 (pages 32–33)

1 **d** All of the other shapes have two squares and two triangles.
2 **a** All of the other shapes have one small white circle.
3 **e** All of the other shapes have the three rectangles positioned to give a U-shape.
4 **d**
5 **d**
6 **d**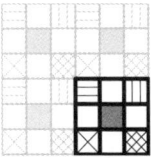
7 **e** The patterns within each quarter of the grid are identical.
8 **c** The bottom right of the grid is a reflection of the top left pattern, when reflected in a diagonal mirror line from bottom left to top right.
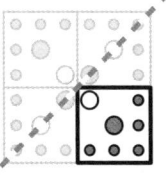
9 **b** The bottom right of the grid is a reflection of the top left pattern, when reflected in a diagonal mirror line from bottom left to top right.
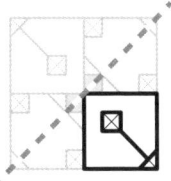
10 **e** The first letter represents the position and orientation of the triangle (J is below circle with flat base, L is above circle with flat base, K is above circle with point at the base, M is below circle with point at the base); the second letter represents the shading in the triangle (B is horizontal lines, D is solid grey, C is cross-hatch, A is vertical lines).
11 **c** The first letter represents the position of the grey circle (A is top left, B is top centre, C is top right and D is bottom centre); the second letter represents the direction of the arrow (P is north-east, R is south, S is north-west, Q is east).
12 **d** The first letter represents the number of beads on the thread (Z is 7, Y is 6, X is 5); the second letter represents the pattern in the small square (A is blank, B is single line bottom left to top right, C is single line top left to bottom right, D is a cross).

## Test 17 (pages 34–35)

1 **e** The shape is rotated 90° clockwise, with the shapes at the end of the lines switching.
2 **c** The missing shape fits like a jigsaw piece. It is the outline of a circle overlapping the top right corner of a square on a rectangular base.
3 **d** The first 'upside down flag' in the shape is flipped to be the right way up, the second is flipped to point to the right rather than the left, The two flags are touching.
4 **c**
5 **d**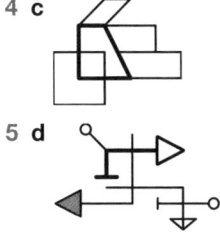

6 e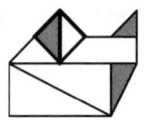

7 c All of the other shapes have two different sized angles between the three projecting lines.
8 b All of the other shapes have a plain white circle at one end.
9 e All of the other shapes have the vertical line ending on the top one of the two short horizontal lines at the base.
10 a The two faces with arrows are on opposite sides of the cube, they cannot be on adjacent faces.
11 d The grey face and the face with the wavy lines are on opposite sides of the cube, they cannot be on adjacent faces.
12 c When the face with three spots is at the top and the grey face at the front, the face to the right would be an inverted triangle, not the squared shaded face.

## Test 18 (pages 36–37)

1 c The circles change to rhombuses; the white half of each shape becomes shaded and the shaded part unshaded.
2 e The short line at the base changes to a white triangle and the lines projecting at right angles become lines projecting in the same direction but separated by acute angles.
3 b The circles in a column change to be within a larger oval, keeping the same shading patterns and the same number of short lines coming from the column cross the perimeter of the oval shape.
4 e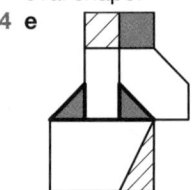
5 c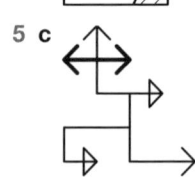
6 d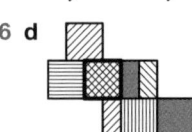

7 e (refer to Test 8 Q1–6 reflections)
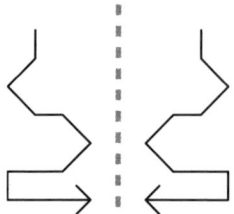

8 c (refer to Test 8 Q1–6 reflections)
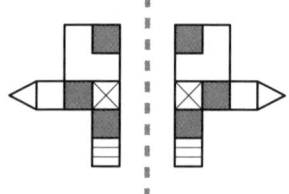

9 d (refer to Test 8 Q1–6 reflections)

10 d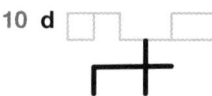

11 e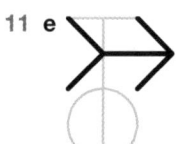

12 b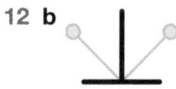

## Test 19 (pages 38–39)

1 c Both the short lines and the white circles follow the pattern 3–2–1–2–3–2–1–etc.
2 e The top zigzag line decreases by one line each time, the bottom zigzag line increases by one line each time.
3 d The large and small T-shapes alternate so the next one must be small. There should be a white circle top middle of the T which only leaves option d.
4 b In all of the other shapes the inner circle has a dotted line inside the solid circle.
5 d All of the other shapes have five sides.

6 **e** All of the other shapes have coiled lines but no arrowhead.
7 **d** The first letter represents the shape of the 'envelope' (L a wide rectangle, M a thin rectangle, N a square); the second letter represents the pattern on the envelope (A a white square, B a black square, C the wavy lines and D a wide V-shape).
8 **b** The first letter represents the number of grey circles (A is 4, B is 3, C is 2 and D is 1); the second letter represents the number of ovals crossing the outline (X is 3, Y is 2 and Z is 3).
9 **e** The first letter represents the style of circle shading (P horizontal lines, Q cross-hatch lines, R black); the second letter represents the location of the triangle on the outside (S is top left, T is top right, U is bottom right, V is bottom left).
10 **b**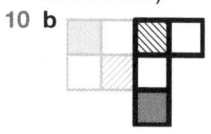

11 **c**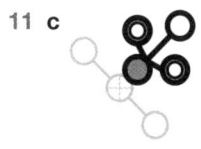

12 **a**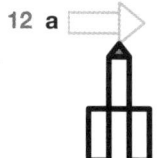

## Test 20 (pages 40–41)

1 **e** The orientation of the triangle alternates; the inner shape alternates between circle and square, with each circle–square pair having the same style of line.
2 **a** The triangle alternates between black and white and the number of white circles increases by one each time always in the same direction.
3 **b** The arrow moves around the square taking two steps along each side and the shaded small square moves clockwise around the central square.
4 **d**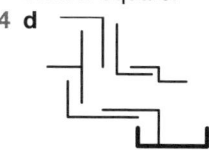

5 **e**

6 **b**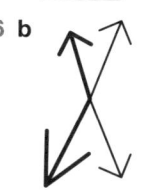

7 **a** (refer to Test 8 Q1–6 reflections)
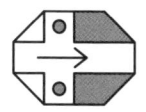

8 **c** (refer to Test 8 Q1–6 reflections)
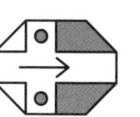

9 **e** (refer to Test 8 Q1–6 reflections)
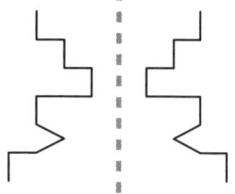

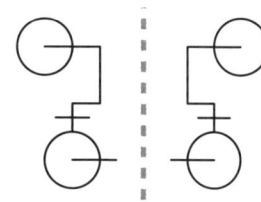

10 **c** When the face with the black circle is at the top and the arrow at the front, the face to the right will have three vertical lines.
11 **e** The arrow, X and triangle faces are in a line in the net so cannot form a corner of the cube.
12 **b** The face with the grey circle and the face with the X must be opposite, not adjacent, in the cube.

## Puzzle 1

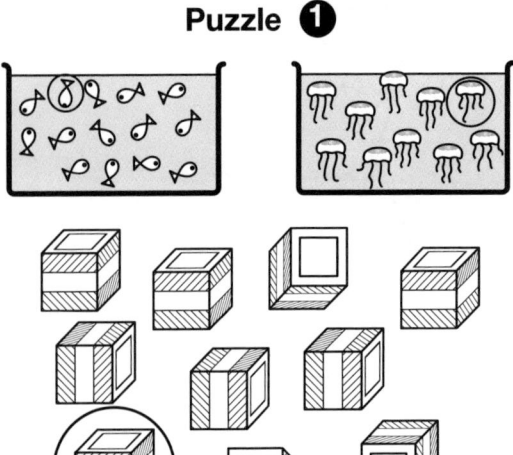

## Puzzle 4

## Puzzle 2

1 **X** 5     2 **X** 7
  **Y** 8           **Y** 2
  **Z** 3           **Z** 5

## Puzzle 3

## Puzzle 5

Which shape or pattern completes the larger grid?

7   a   b   c   d   e

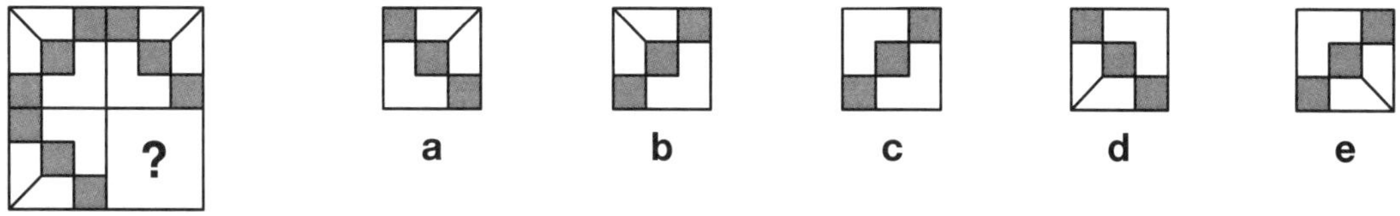

8   a   b   c   d   e

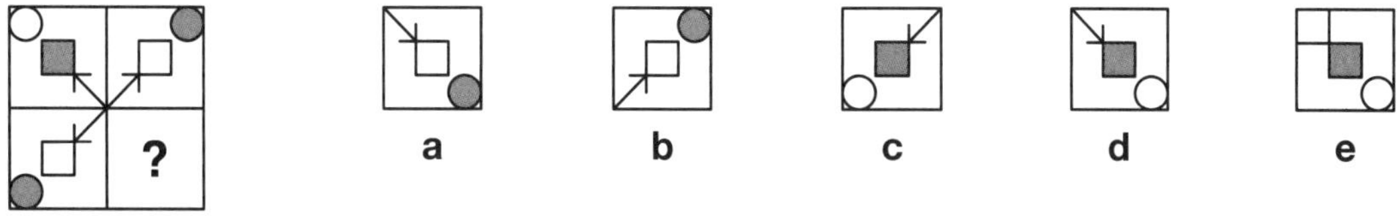

9   a   b   c   d   e

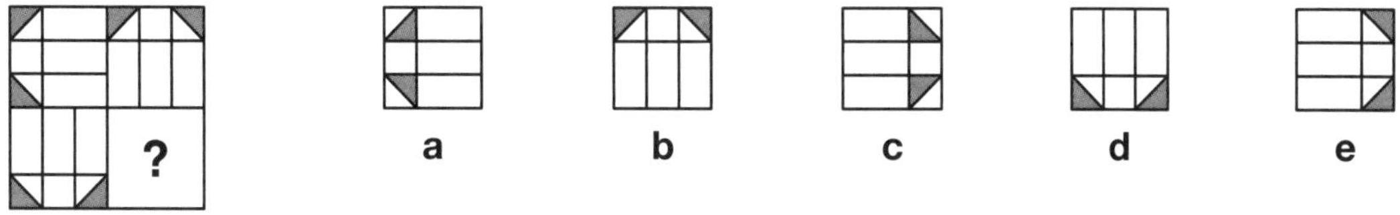

Which shape on the right is the reflection of the shape given on the left?

10   a   b   c   d   e

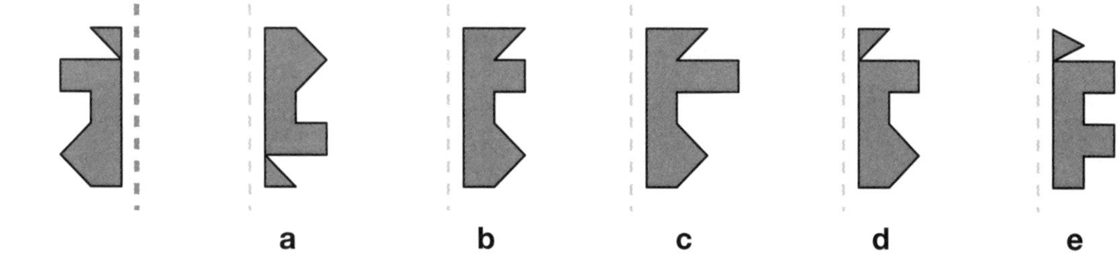

11   a   b   c   d   e

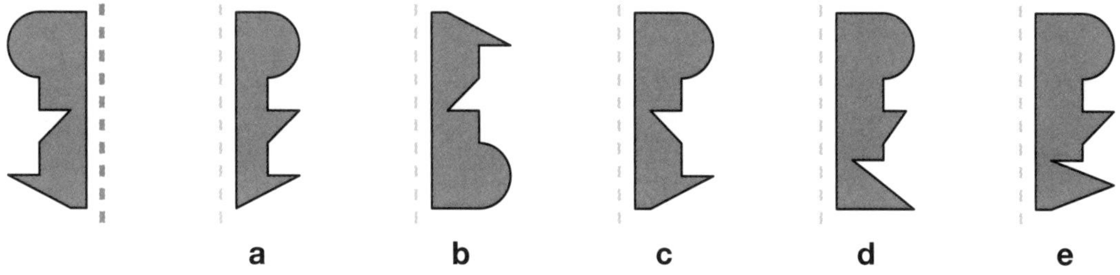

12   a   b   c   d   e

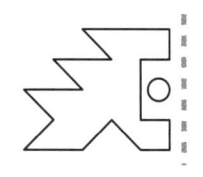

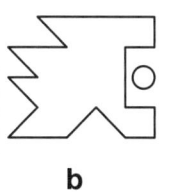

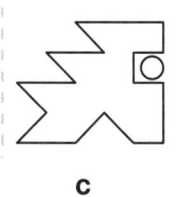

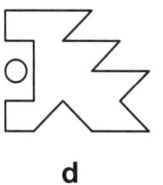

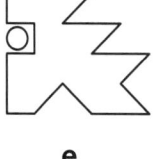

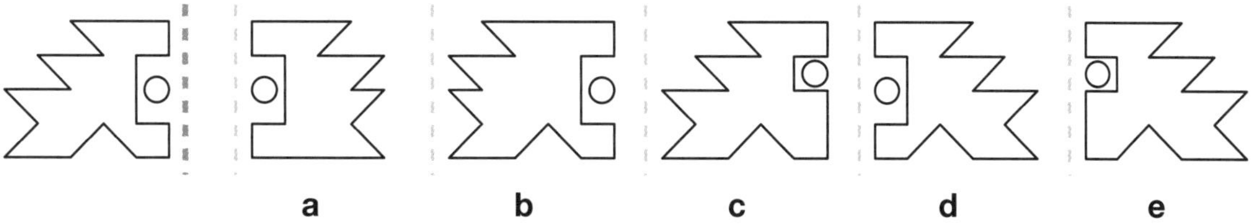

*Time for a break! Go to Puzzle Page 44*

Total

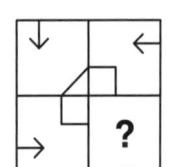

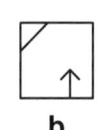

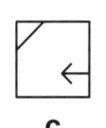

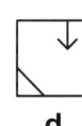

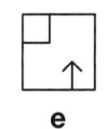

# Test 13: Mixed

Test time: 0–10 minutes

## Which one comes next?

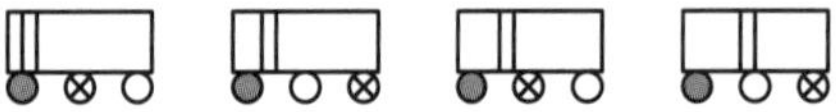

1.

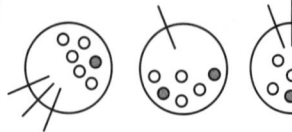

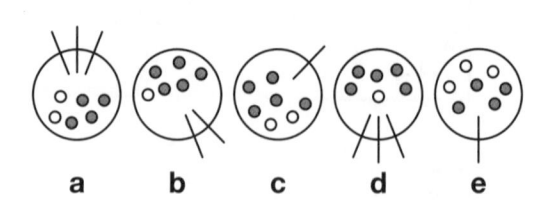

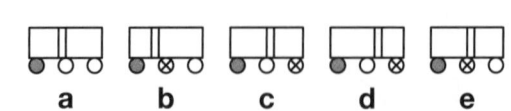

2.

3.

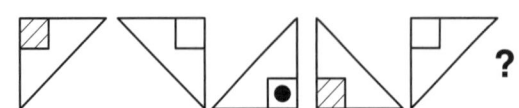

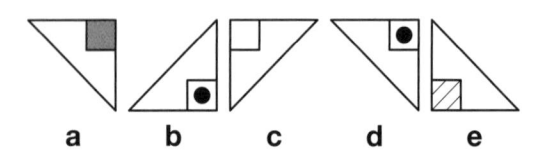

## Which shape or pattern completes the larger grid?

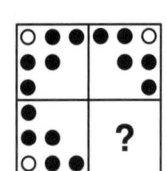

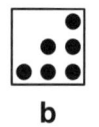

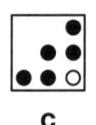

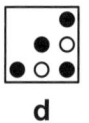

4.

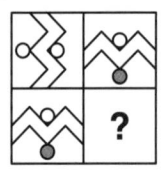

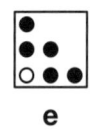

5.

6.

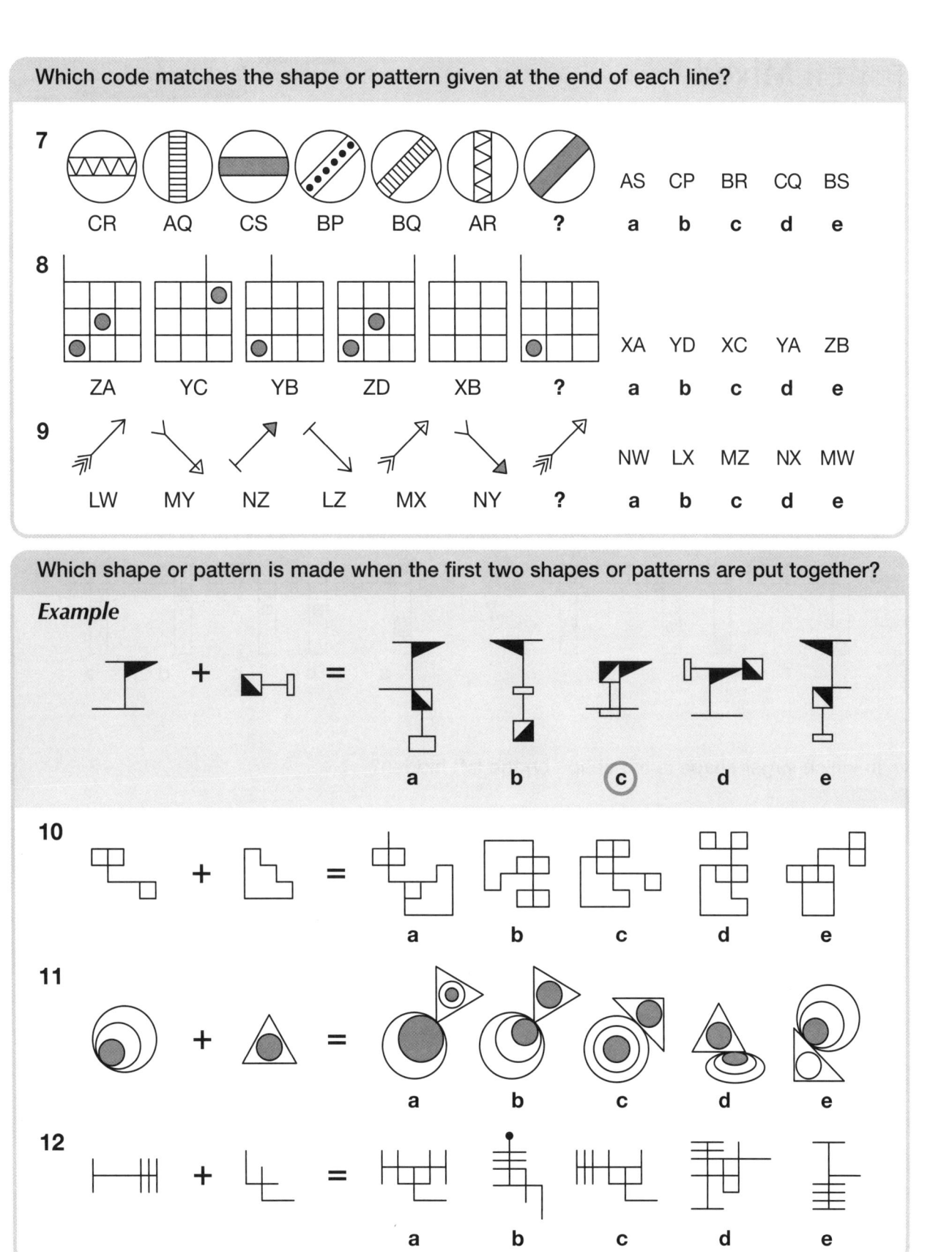

Which code matches the shape or pattern given at the end of each line?

**7** CR  AQ  CS  BP  BQ  AR  ?     AS  CP  BR  CQ  BS
                                    a   b   c   d   e

**8** ZA  YC  YB  ZD  XB  ?          XA  YD  XC  YA  ZB
                                    a   b   c   d   e

**9** LW  MY  NZ  LZ  MX  NY  ?      NW  LX  MZ  NX  MW
                                    a   b   c   d   e

Which shape or pattern is made when the first two shapes or patterns are put together?

*Example*

a  b  **c**  d  e

**10**  a  b  c  d  e

**11**  a  b  c  d  e

**12**  a  b  c  d  e

Total

## Test 14: Mixed

**Which one comes next?**

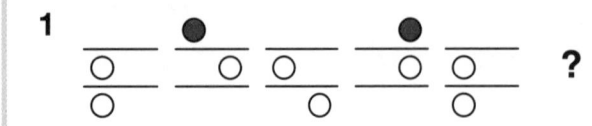

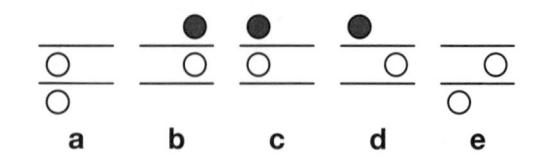

1

2

3

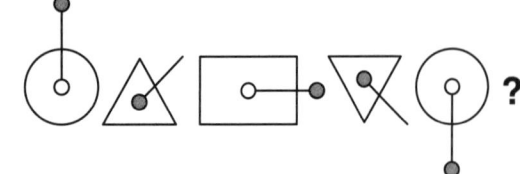

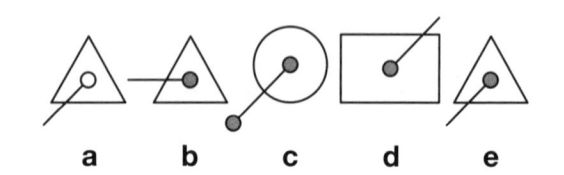

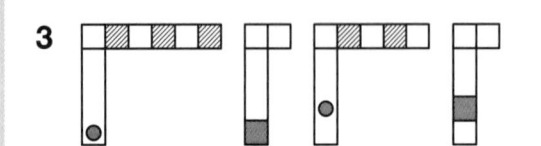

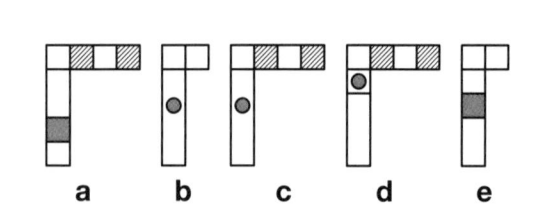

**In which larger shape is the shape on the left hidden?**

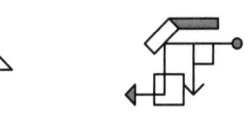

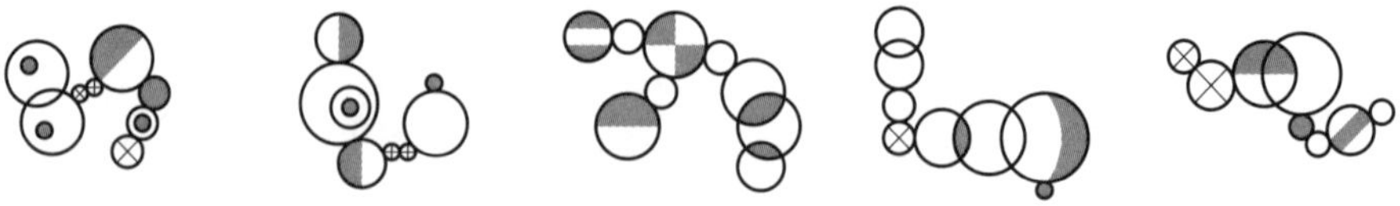

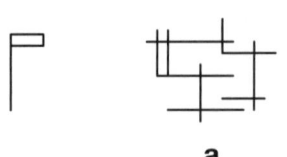

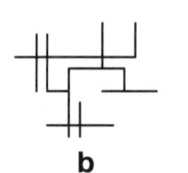

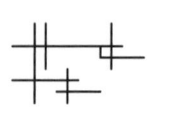

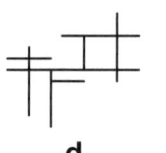

4

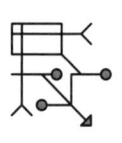

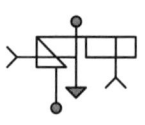

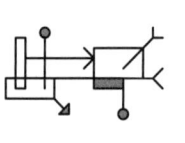

5

6

**Which shape on the right is the reflection of the shape given on the left?**

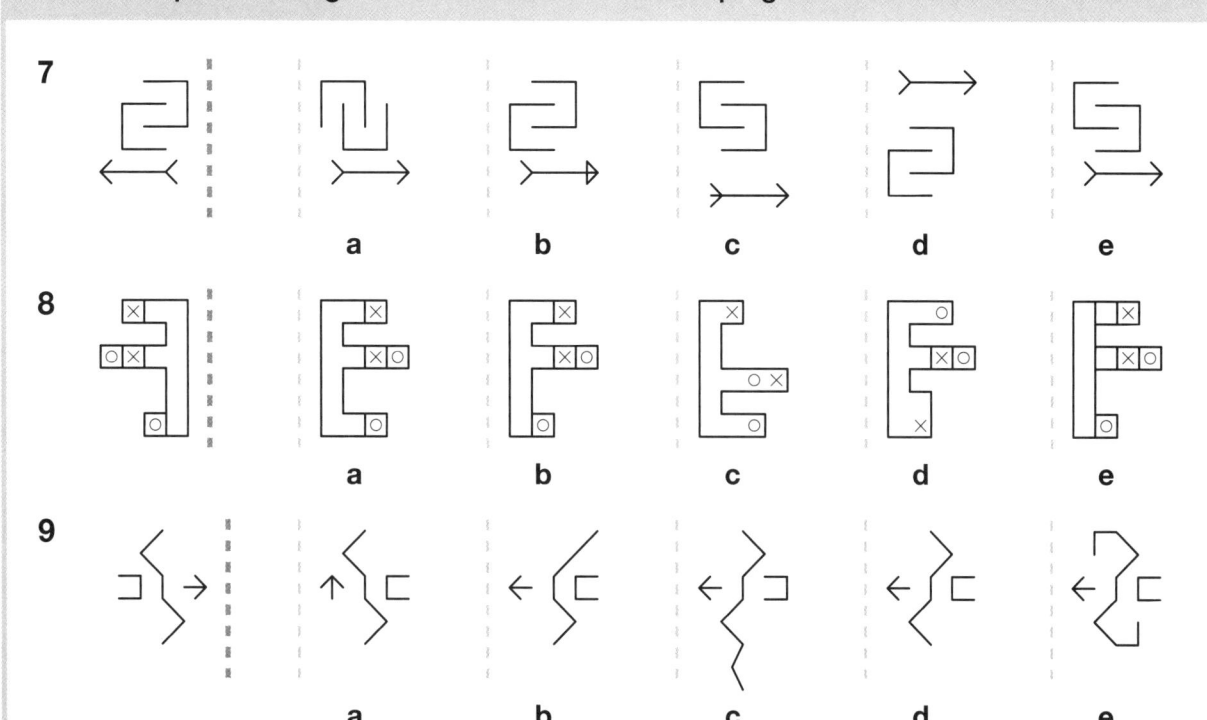

7   a   b   c   d   e

8   a   b   c   d   e

9   a   b   c   d   e

**Which code matches the shape or pattern given at the end of each line?**

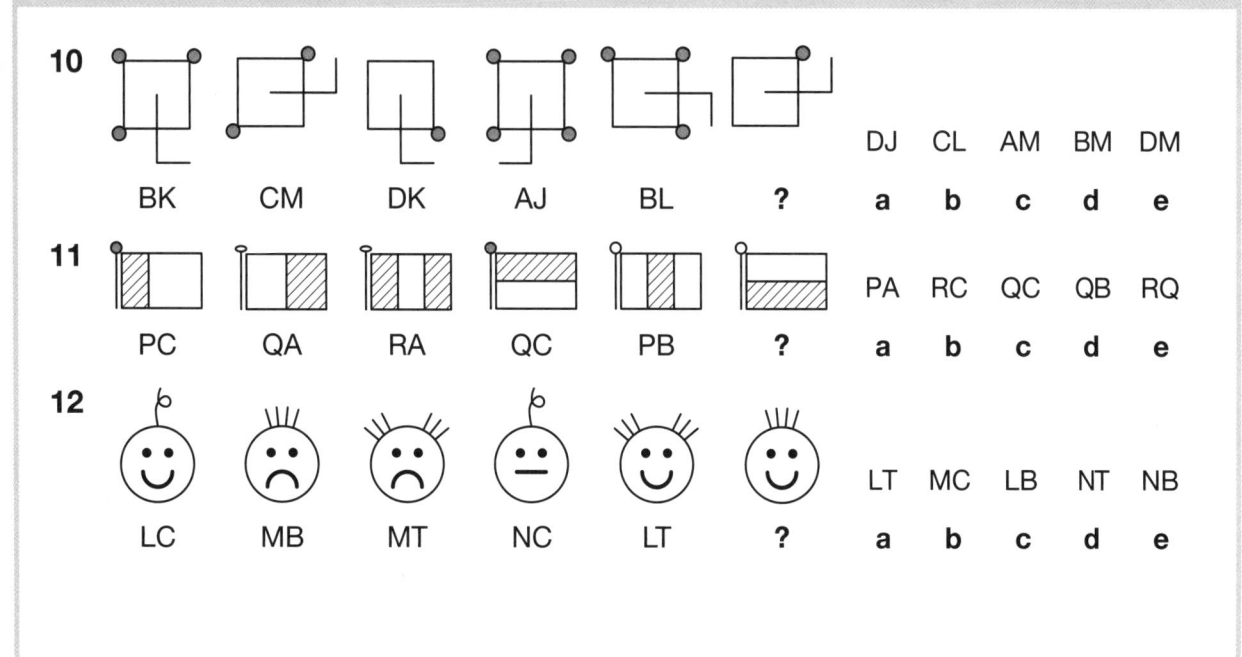

10  BK  CM  DK  AJ  BL  ?     DJ  CL  AM  BM  DM
                               a   b   c   d   e

11  PC  QA  RA  QC  PB  ?     PA  RC  QC  QB  RQ
                               a   b   c   d   e

12  LC  MB  MT  NC  LT  ?     LT  MC  LB  NT  NB
                               a   b   c   d   e

TEST 15: **Mixed**

Test time: 0 — 5 — 10 minutes

Which one comes next?

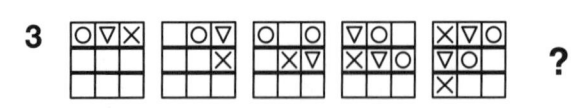

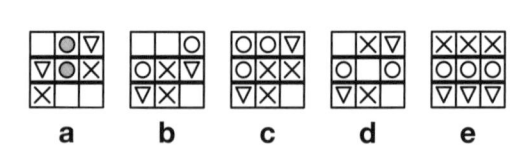

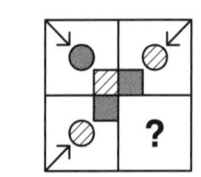

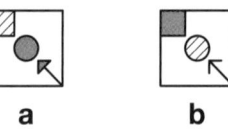

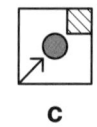

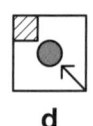

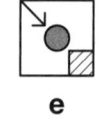

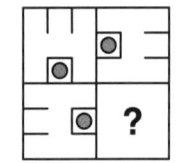

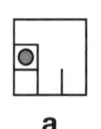

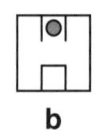

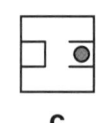

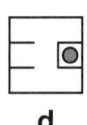

1

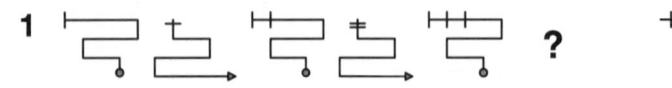

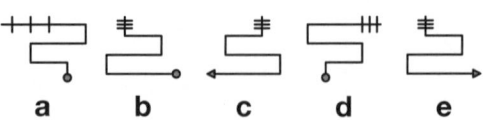

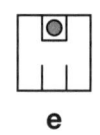

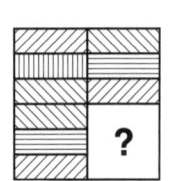

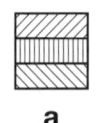

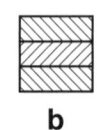

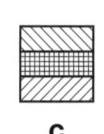

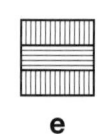

Which shape on the right is the reflection of the shape given on the left?

7

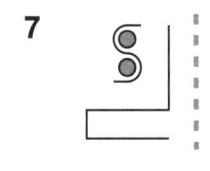

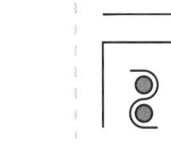

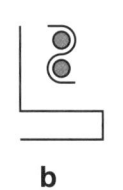

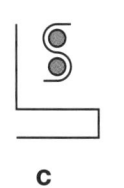

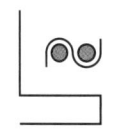

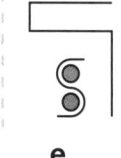

8

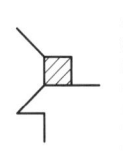

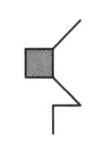

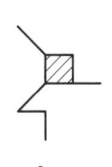

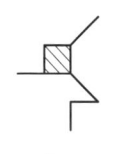

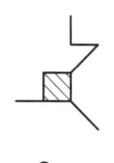

9

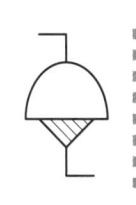

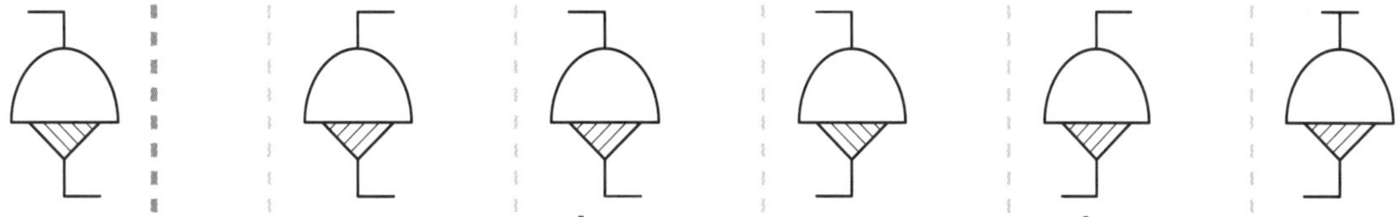

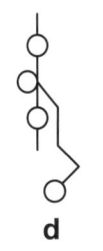

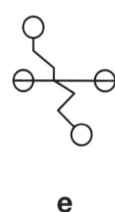

Which shape or pattern is made when the first two shapes or patterns are put together?

10

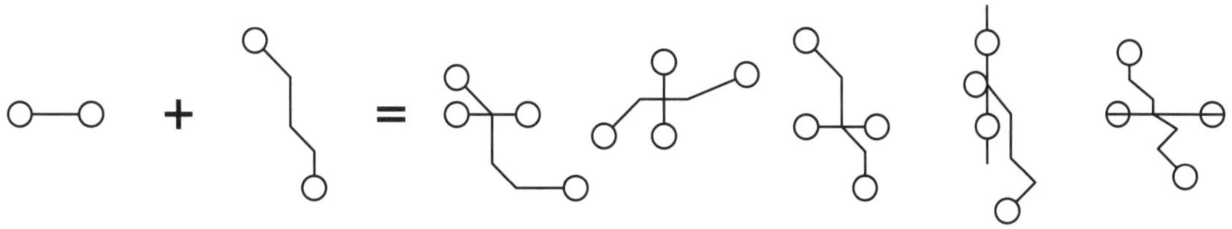

11

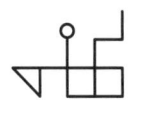

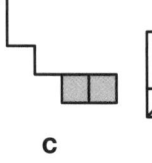

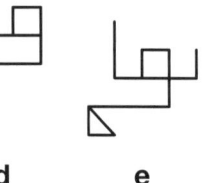

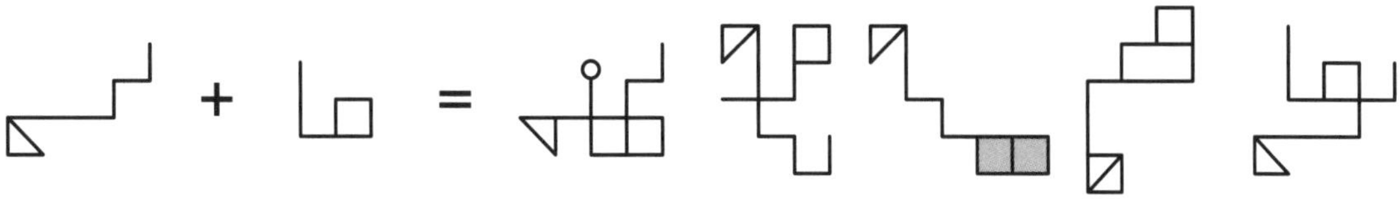

12

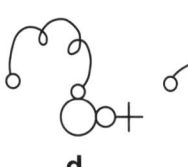

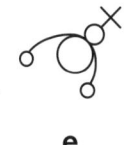

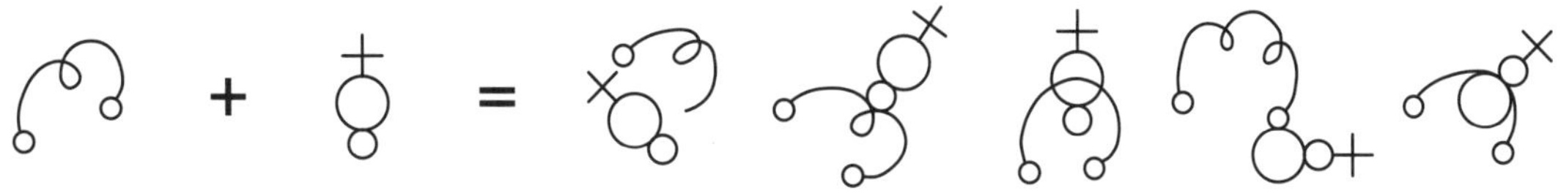

Total

TEST 16: **Mixed**

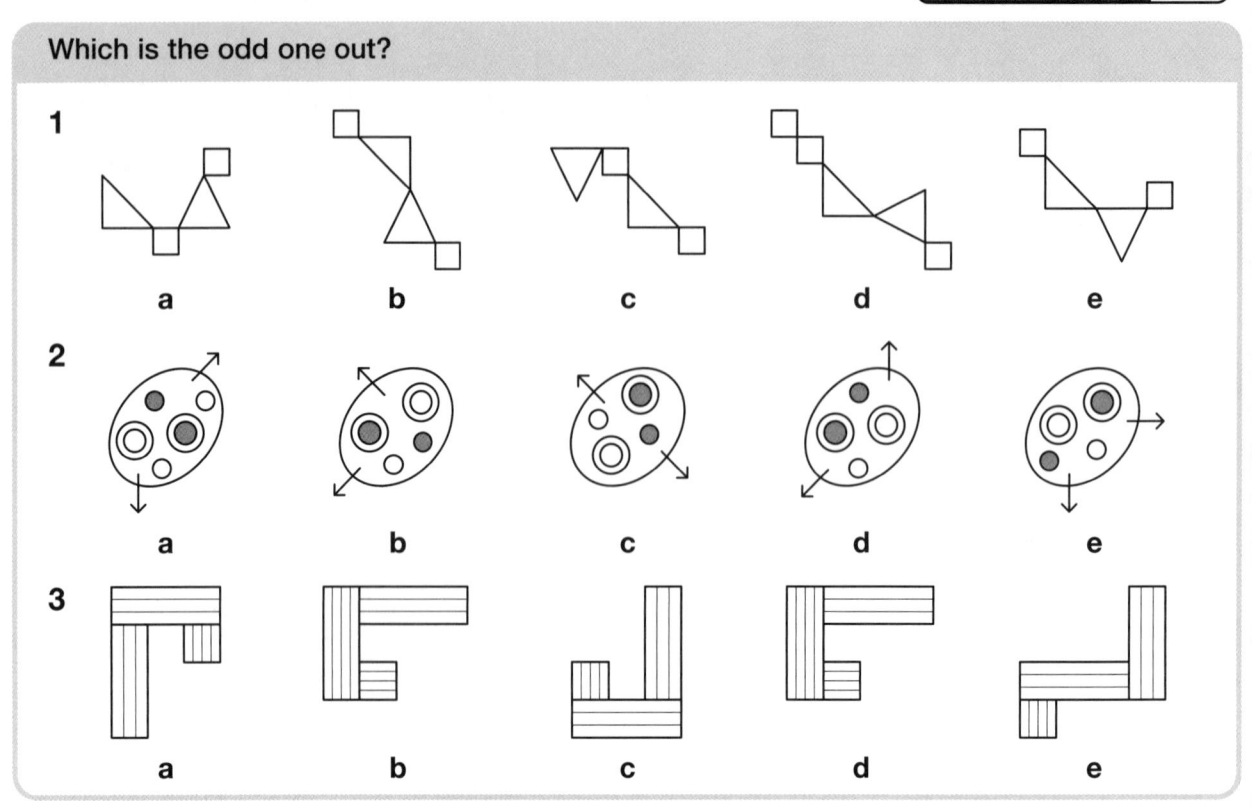

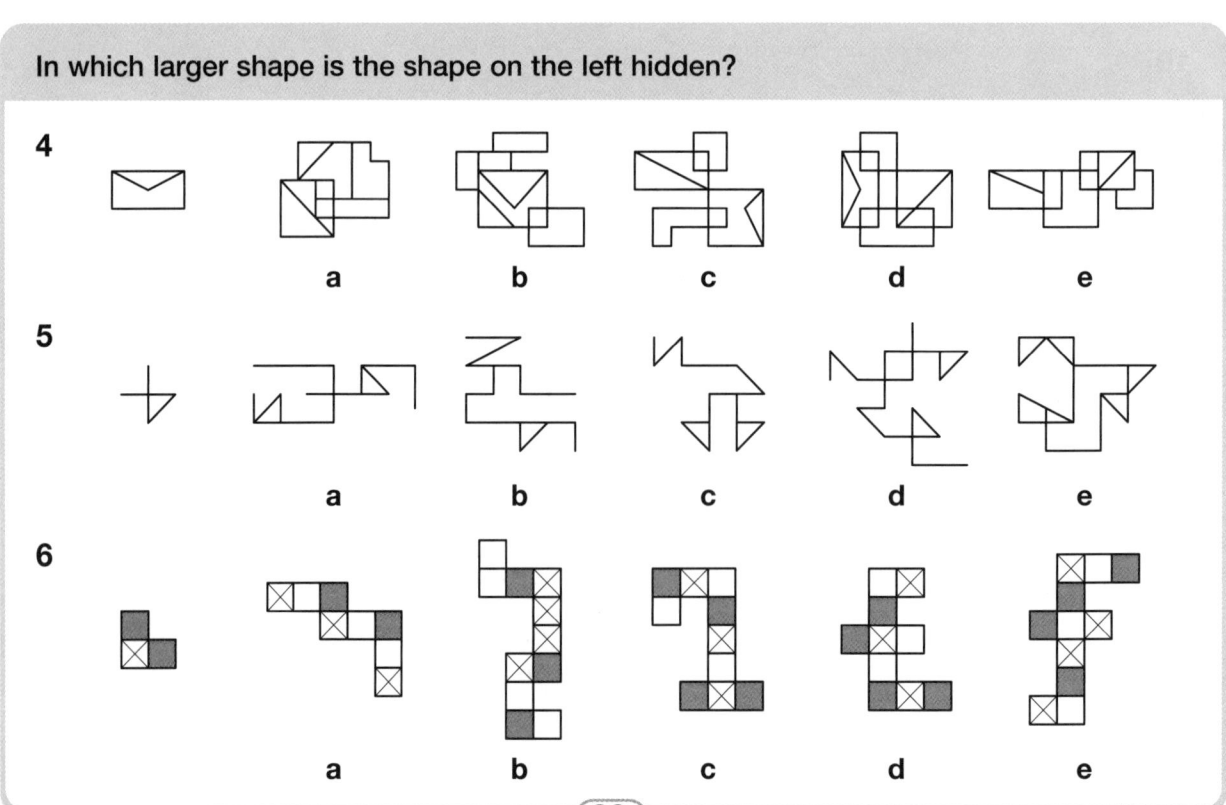

Test time: 0 — 5 — 10 minutes

Which is the odd one out?

1   a   b   c   d   e

2   a   b   c   d   e

3   a   b   c   d   e

In which larger shape is the shape on the left hidden?

4   a   b   c   d   e

5   a   b   c   d   e

6   a   b   c   d   e

Which shape or pattern completes the larger grid?

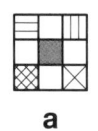

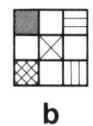

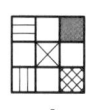

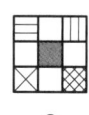

7

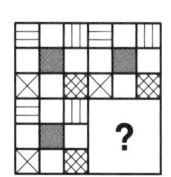

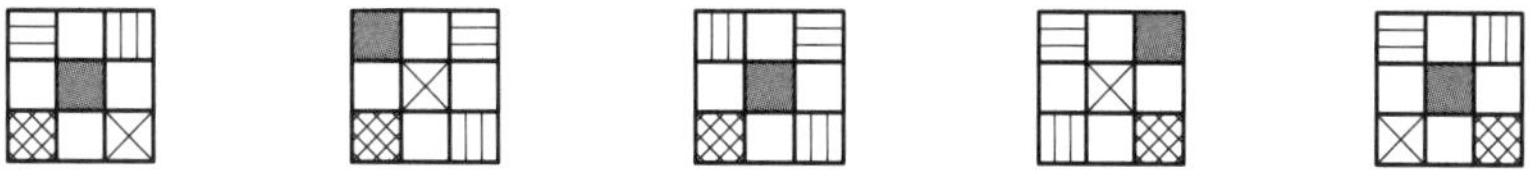

8

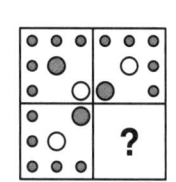

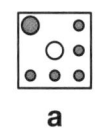

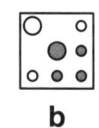

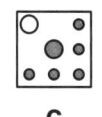

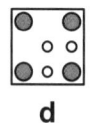

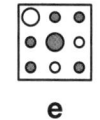

9

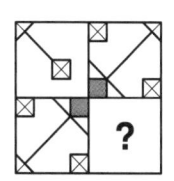

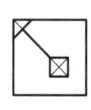

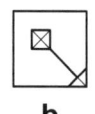

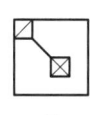

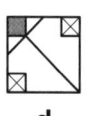

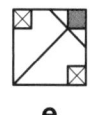

Which code matches the shape or pattern given at the end of each line?

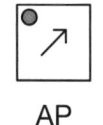

10

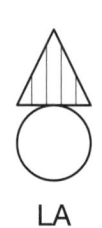

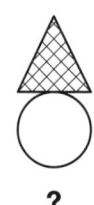

| | LD | JC | KA | MD | LC |
|---|---|---|---|---|---|
| JB | JD | KC | LA | MB | ? |
| | a | b | c | d | e |

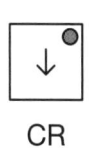

11

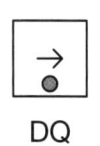

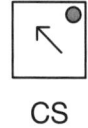

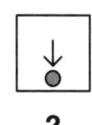

| | DS | AQ | DR | CP | BR |
|---|---|---|---|---|---|
| AP | CR | BS | DQ | CS | ? |
| | a | b | c | d | e |

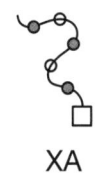

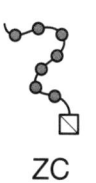

12

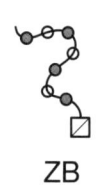

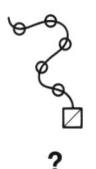

| | XD | YB | ZA | XB | XC |
|---|---|---|---|---|---|
| ZB | YC | XA | ZC | YD | ? |
| | a | b | c | d | e |

*Time for a break! Go to Puzzle Page 45*

# Test 17: Mixed

Test time: 0 — 5 — 10 minutes

**Which shape or pattern completes the second pair in the same way as the first pair?**

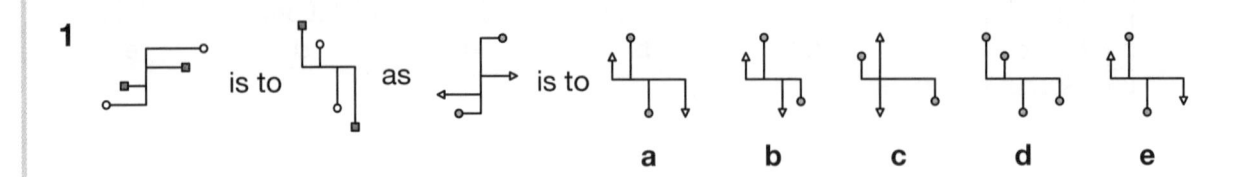

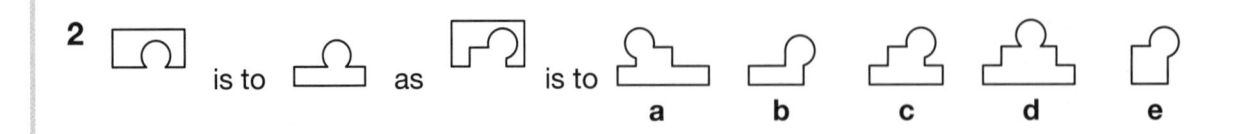

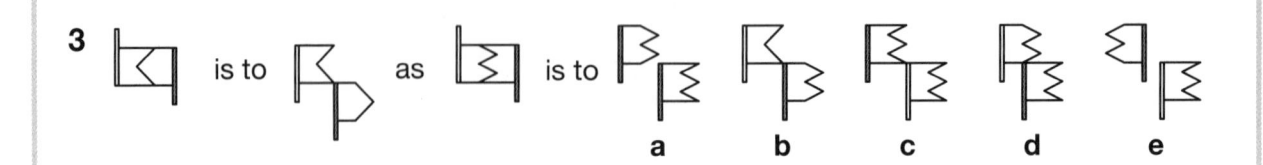

1. is to — as — is to — a  b  c  d  e

2. is to — as — is to — a  b  c  d  e

3. is to — as — is to — a  b  c  d  e

**In which larger shape is the shape on the left hidden?**

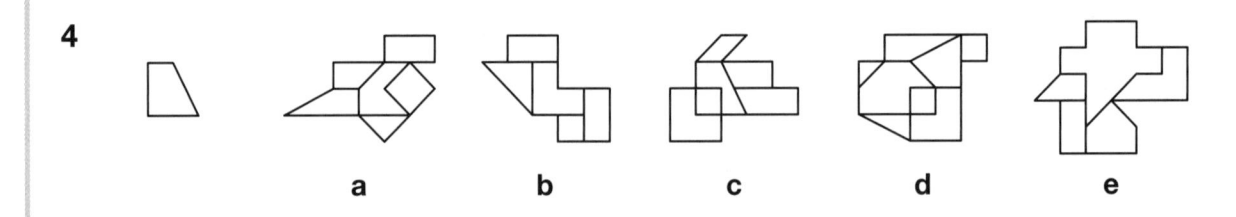

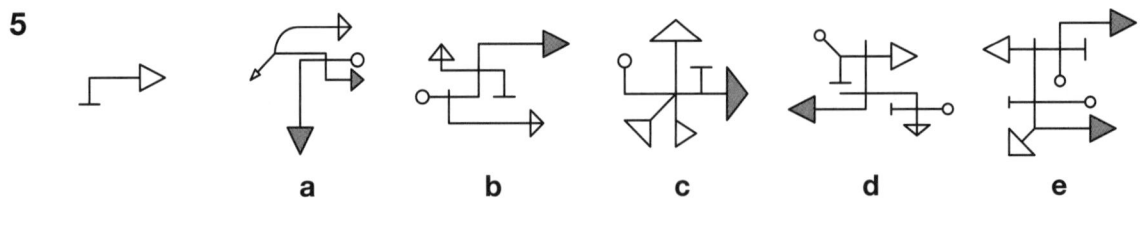

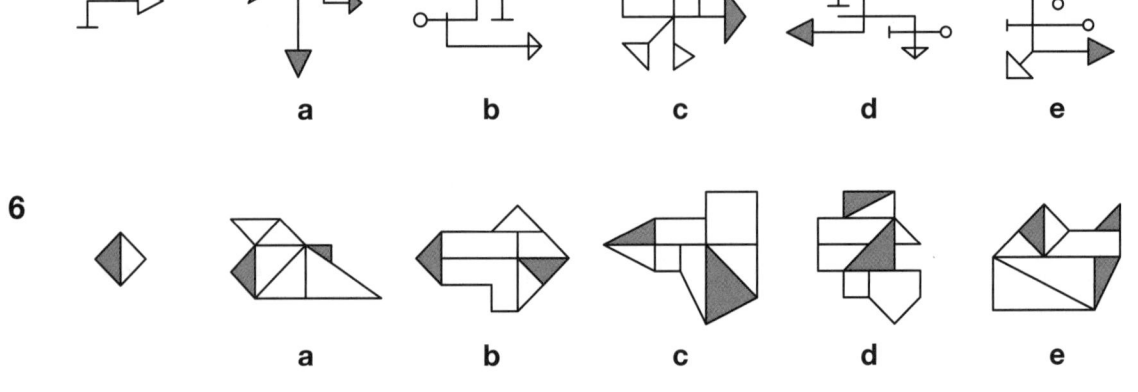

4. a  b  c  d  e

5. a  b  c  d  e

6. a  b  c  d  e

Which is the odd one out?

7

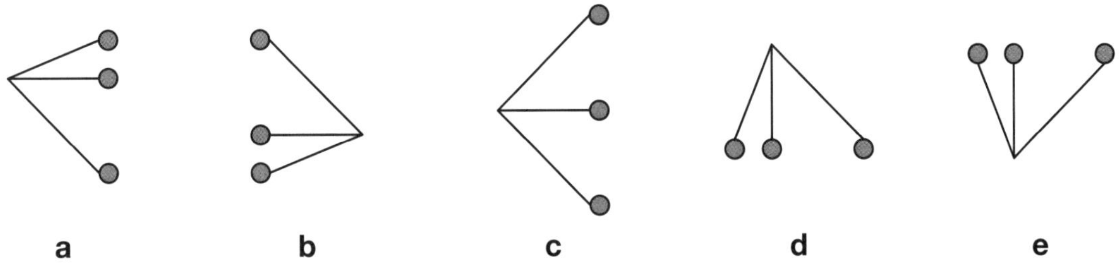

a  b  c  d  e

8

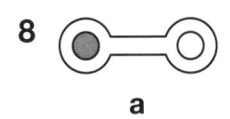

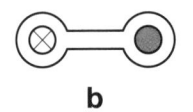

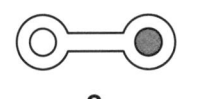

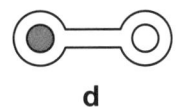

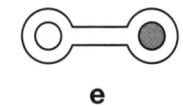

a  b  c  d  e

9

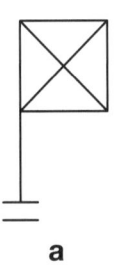

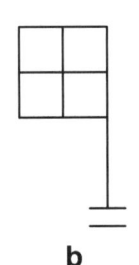

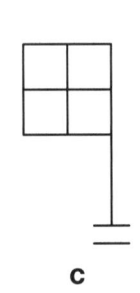

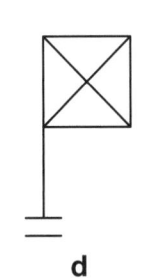

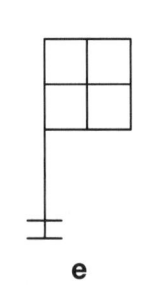

a  b  c  d  e

Which cube cannot be made from the given net?

10

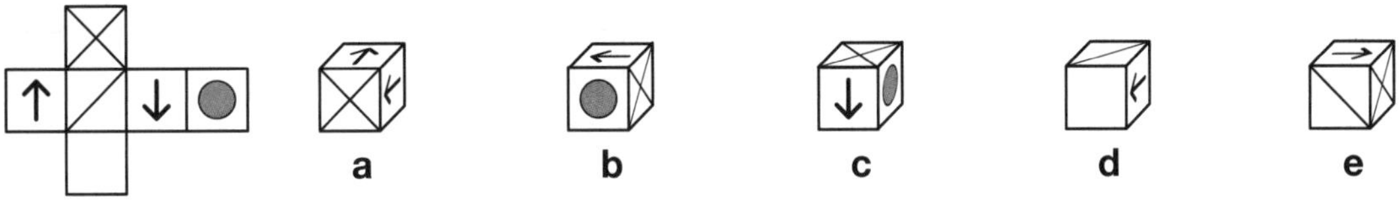

a  b  c  d  e

11

a  b  c  d  e

12

a  b  c  d  e

Total

TEST 18: **Mixed**

Test time: 0 — 5 — 10 minutes

## Which shape or pattern completes the second pair in the same way as the first pair?

**1** is to … as … is to … a b c d e

**2** is to … as … is to … a b c d e

**3** is to … as … is to … a b c d e

## In which larger shape is the shape on the left hidden?

**4** a b c d e

**5** a b c d e

**6** a b c d e

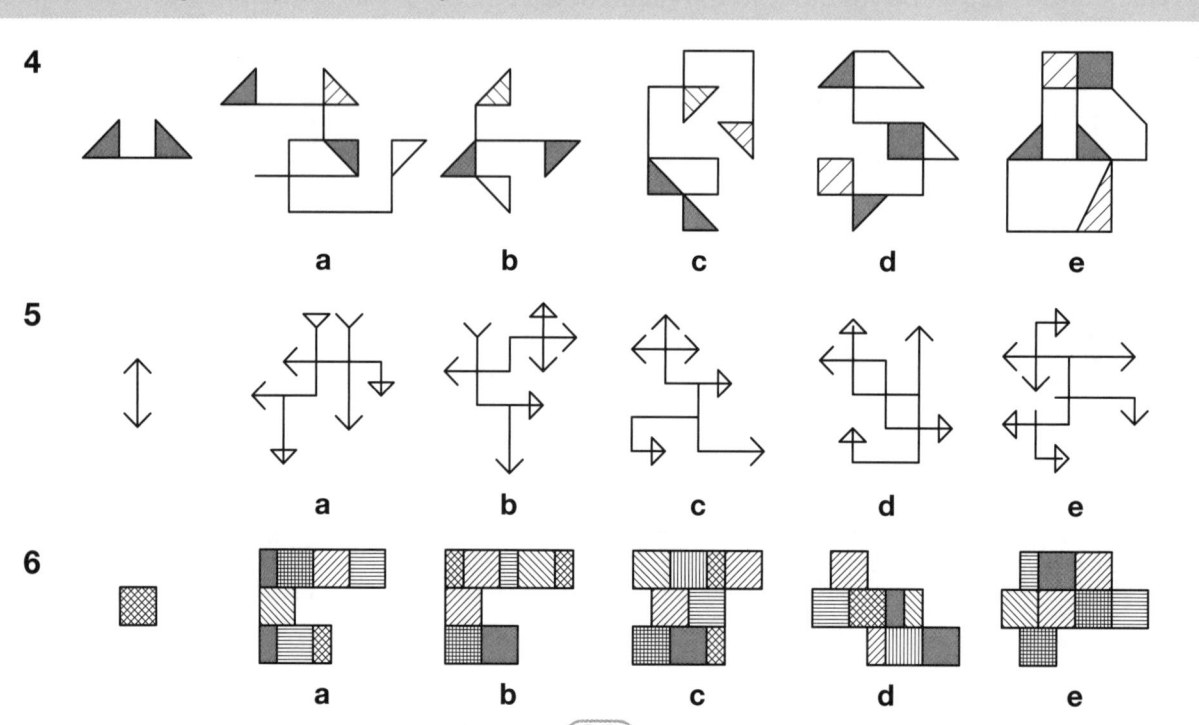

36

Which shape on the right is the reflection of the shape given on the left?

7

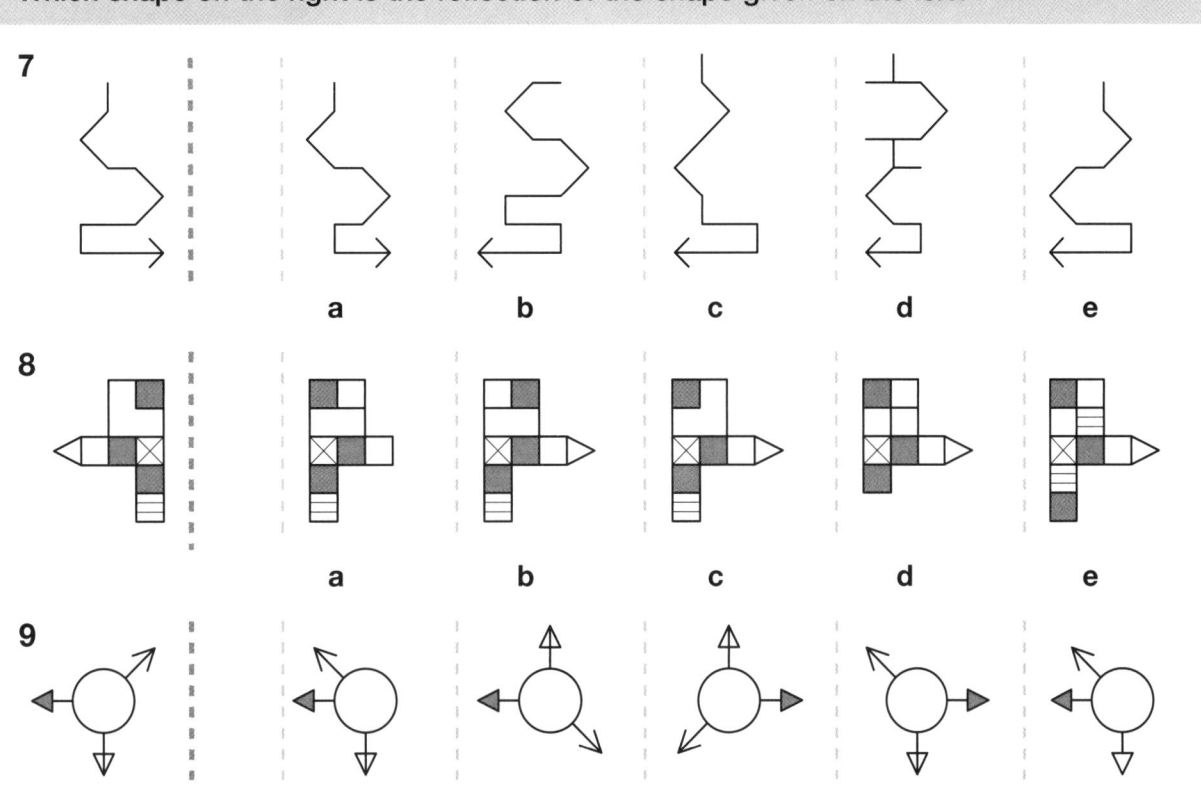

8

9

Which shape or pattern is made when the first two shapes or patterns are put together?

10

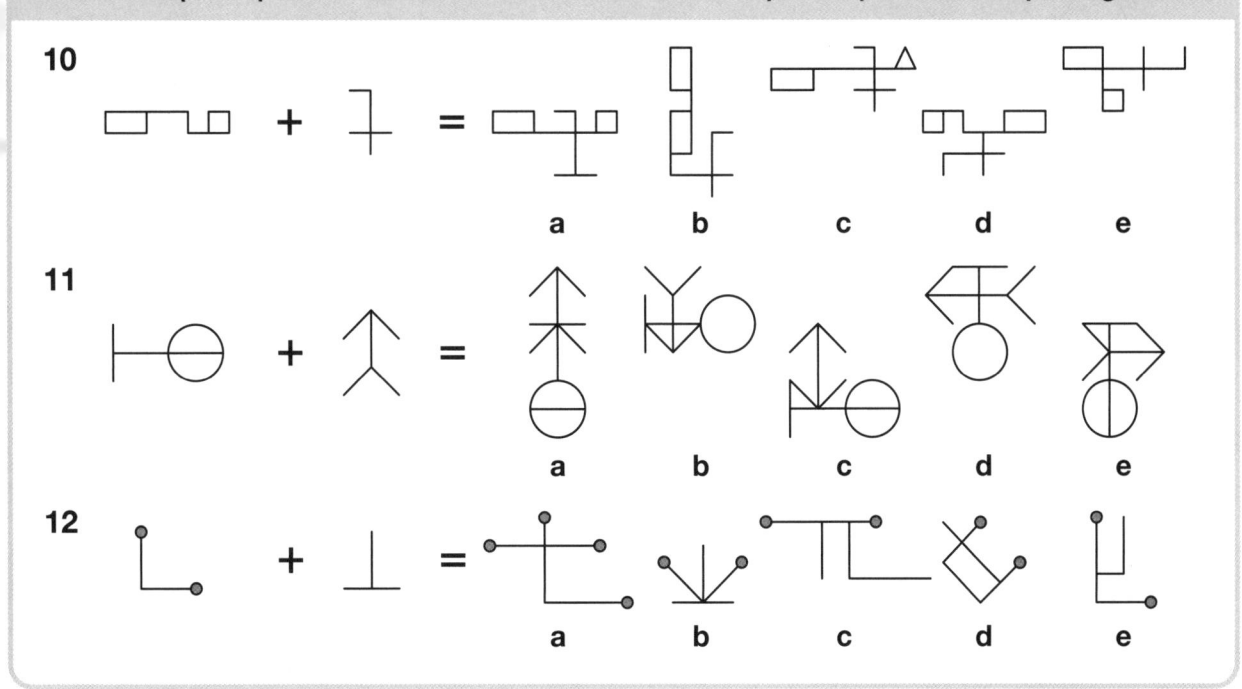

11

12

# Test 19: Mixed

Test time: 0–10 minutes

## Which one comes next?

1.  a  b  c  d  e

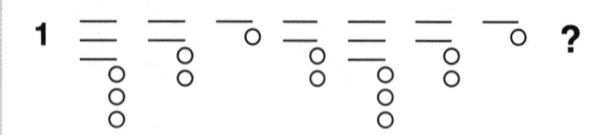

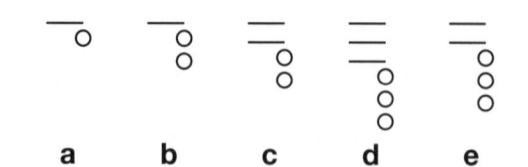

2.  a  b  c  d  e

3.  a  b  c  d  e

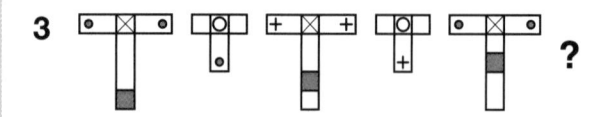

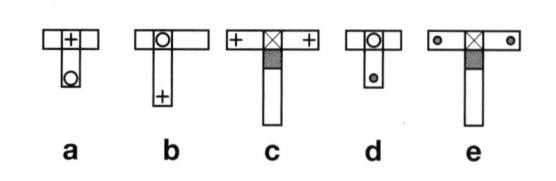

## Which is the odd one out?

4.  a  b  c  d  e

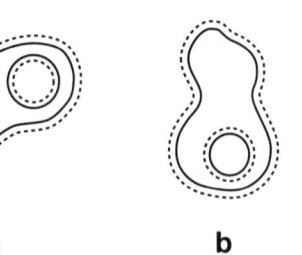

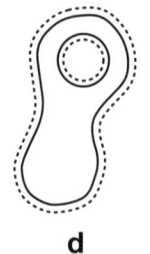

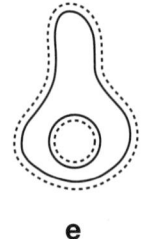

5.  a  b  c  d  e

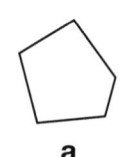

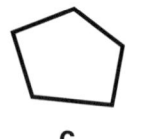

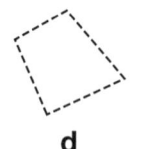

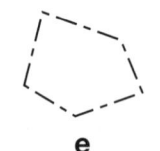

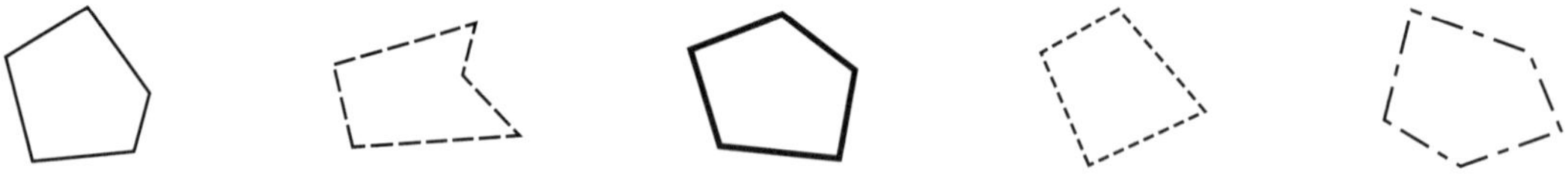

6.  a  b  c  d  e

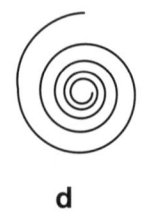

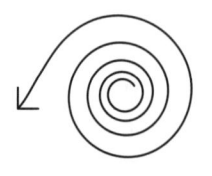

Which code matches the shape or pattern given at the end of each line?

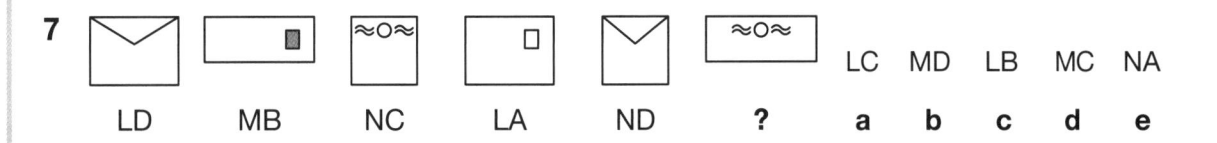

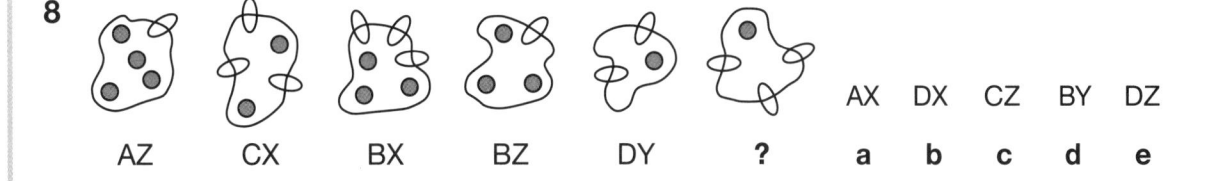

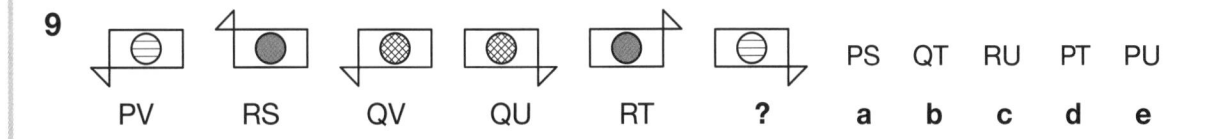

7.   LD   MB   NC   LA   ND   ?      LC   MD   LB   MC   NA
                                      a    b    c    d    e

8.   AZ   CX   BX   BZ   DY   ?      AX   DX   CZ   BY   DZ
                                      a    b    c    d    e

9.   PV   RS   QV   QU   RT   ?      PS   QT   RU   PT   PU
                                      a    b    c    d    e

Which shape or pattern is made when the first two shapes or patterns are put together?

10.   a   b   c   d   e

11.   a   b   c   d   e

12.   a   b   c   d   e

Total

# Test 20: Mixed

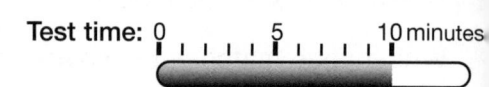

Test time: 0–10 minutes

**Which one comes next?**

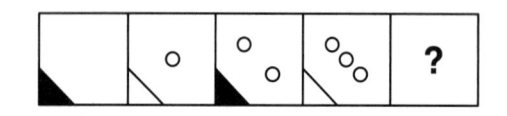

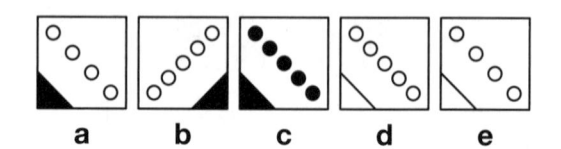

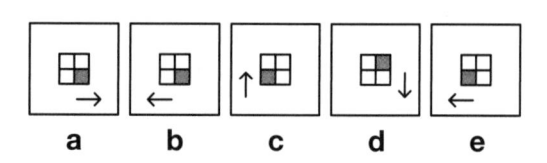

1.
2.
3.

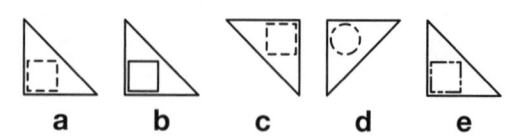

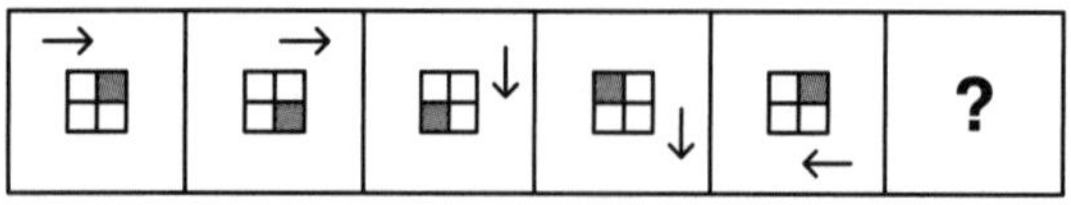

**In which larger shape is the shape on the left hidden?**

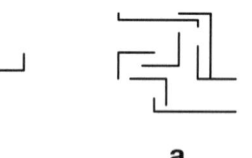

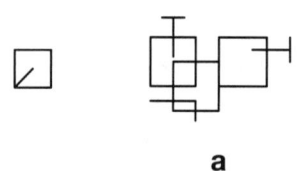

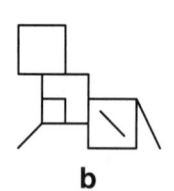

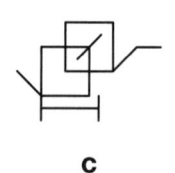

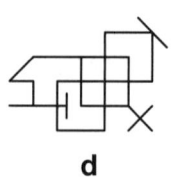

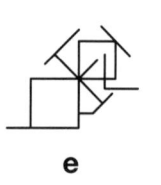

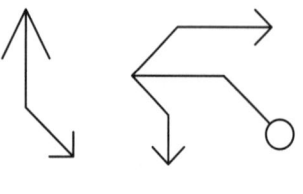

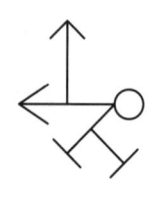

4.
5.
6.

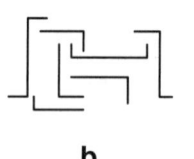

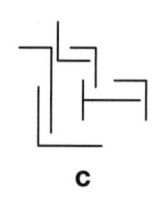

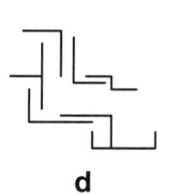

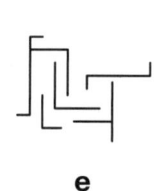

40

Which shape on the right is the reflection of the shape given on the left?

7

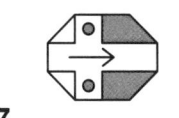

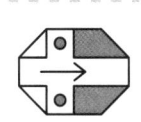

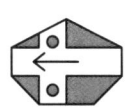

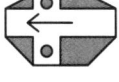

8

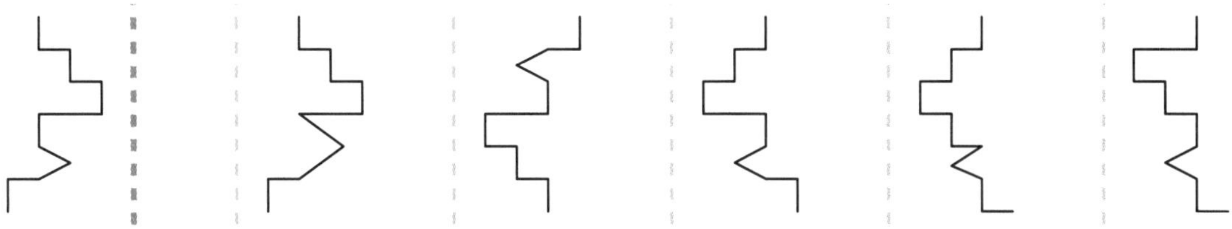

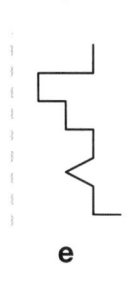

9

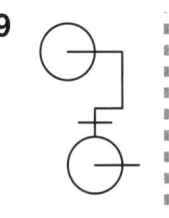

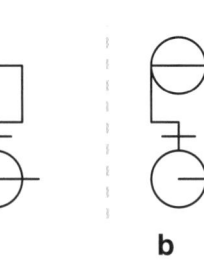

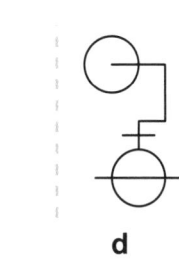

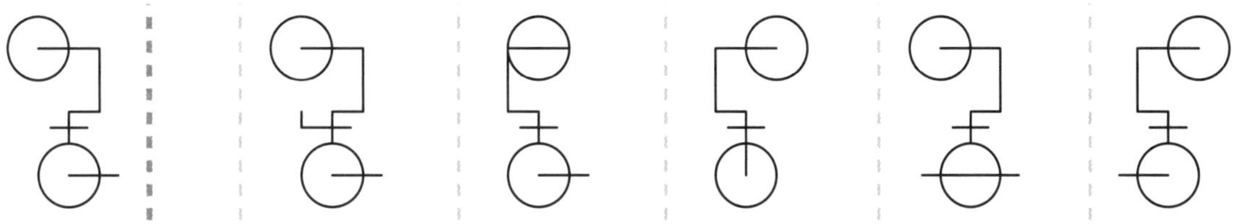

Which cube cannot be made from the given net?

10

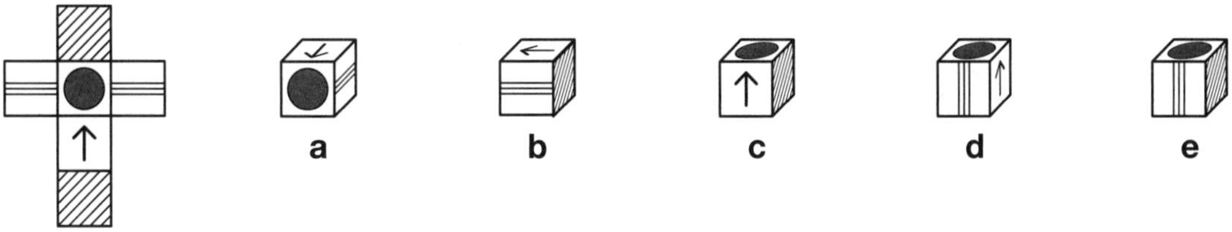

11

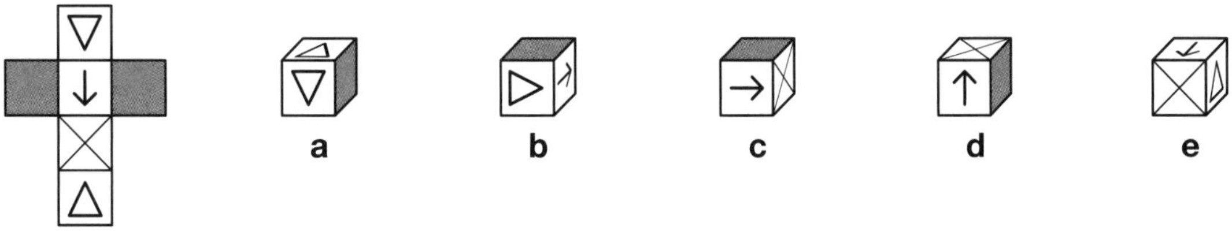

12

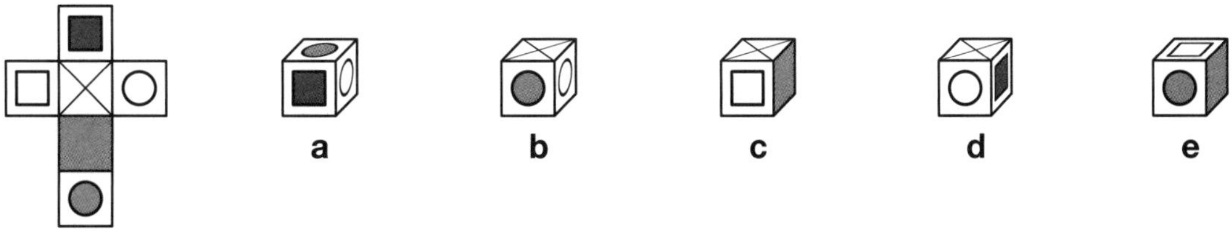

*Time for a break! Go to Puzzle Page 46*

# Puzzle 1

Find the shape in each box that is different from the others.

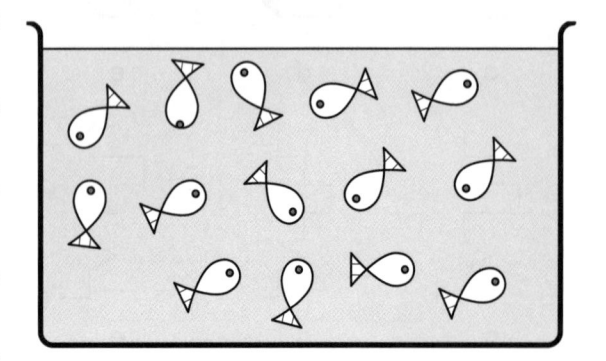

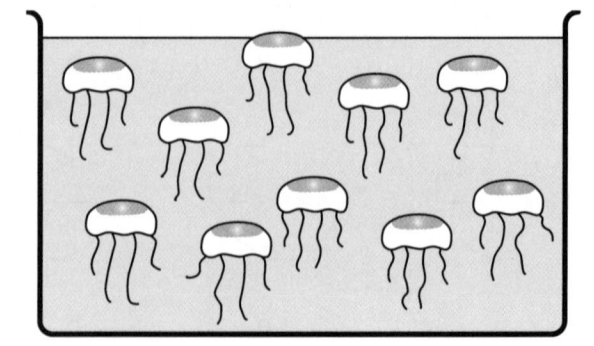

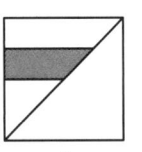

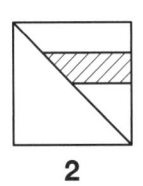

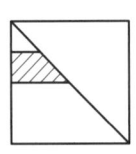

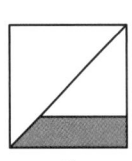

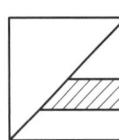

# Puzzle 2

Find the missing puzzle pieces.

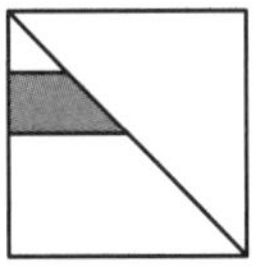

1

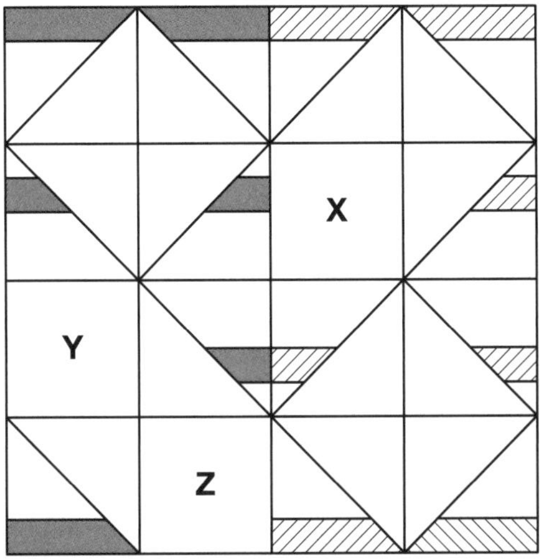

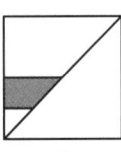

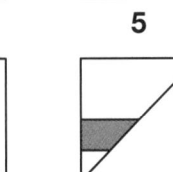

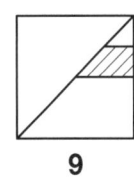

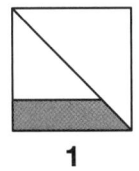

X is _____
Y is _____
Z is _____

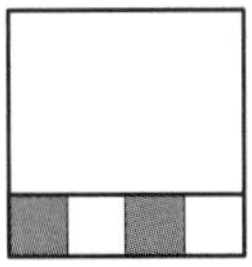

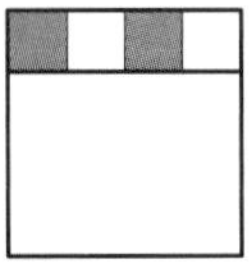

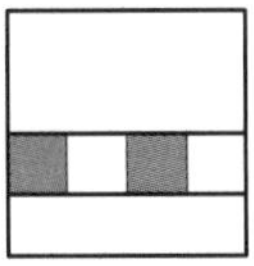

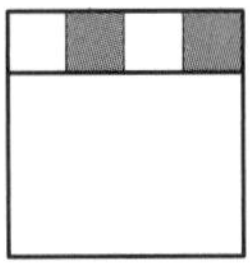

2

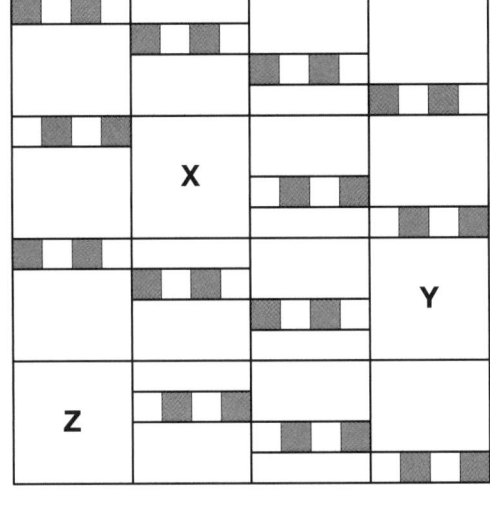

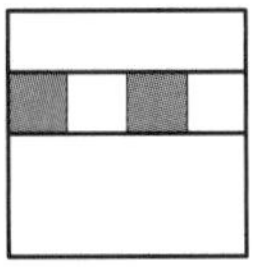

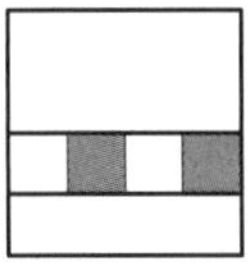

X is _____
Y is _____
Z is _____

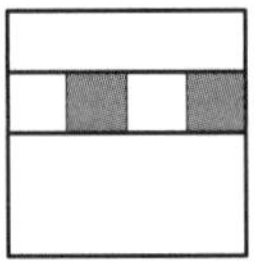

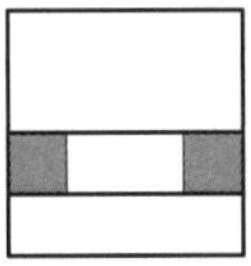

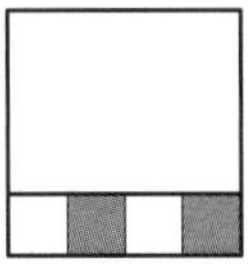

# Puzzle ❸

Match the pattern to its shadow!

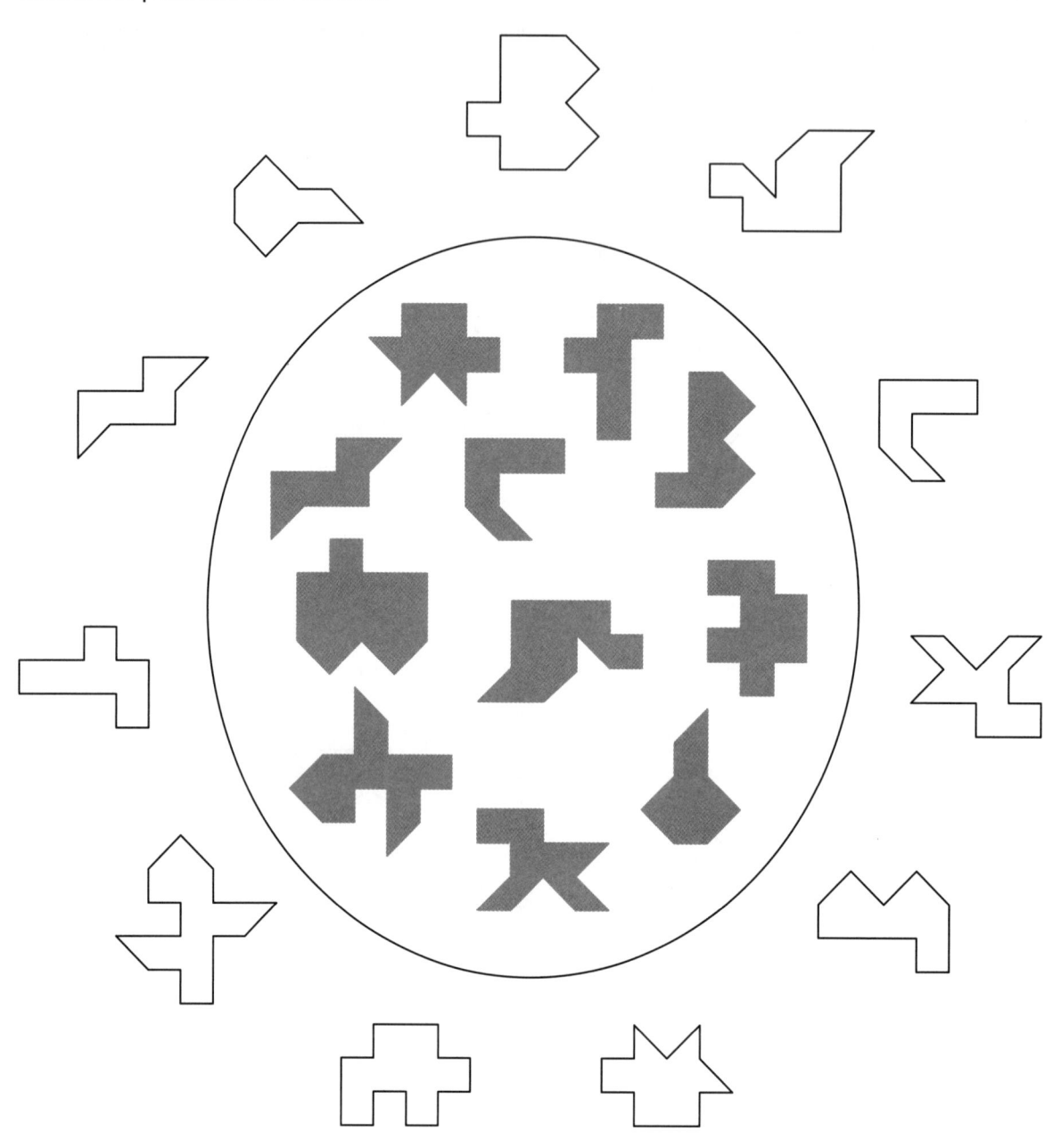

# Puzzle 4

Complete these symmetrical patterns. You may like to colour them in.

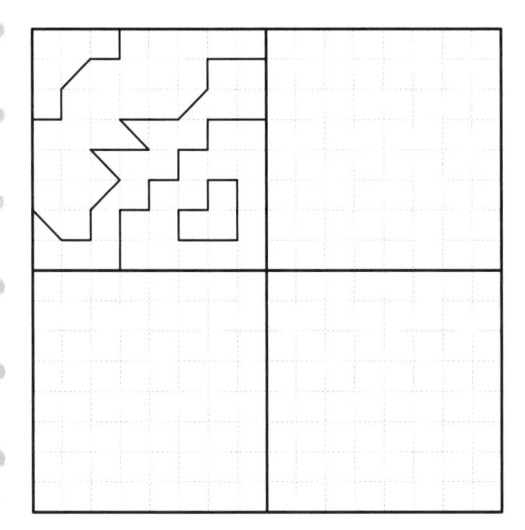

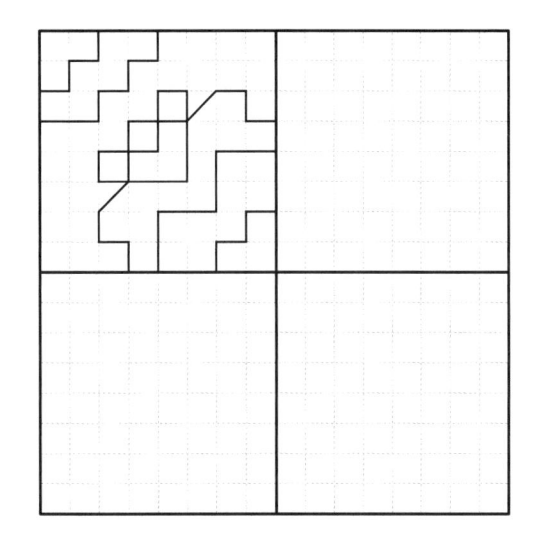

Now make your own symmetrical pattern.

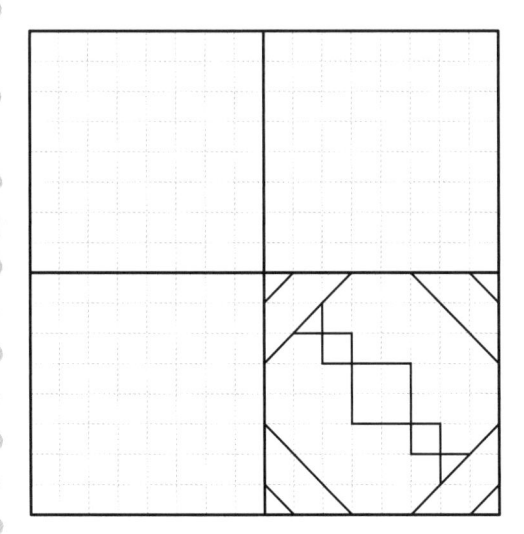

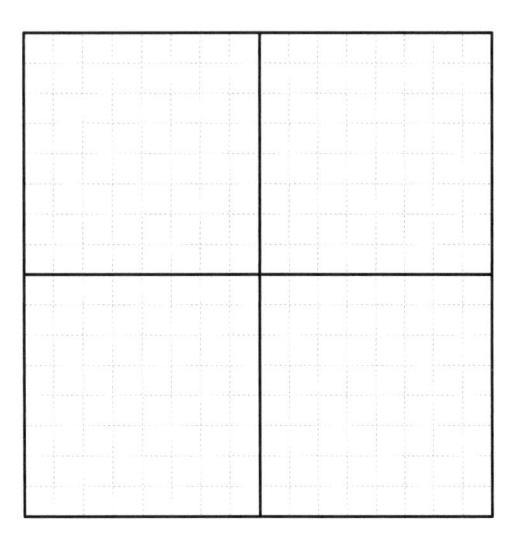

# Puzzle 5

There is a continuing pattern in each of these rows of flags – can you complete the rows?

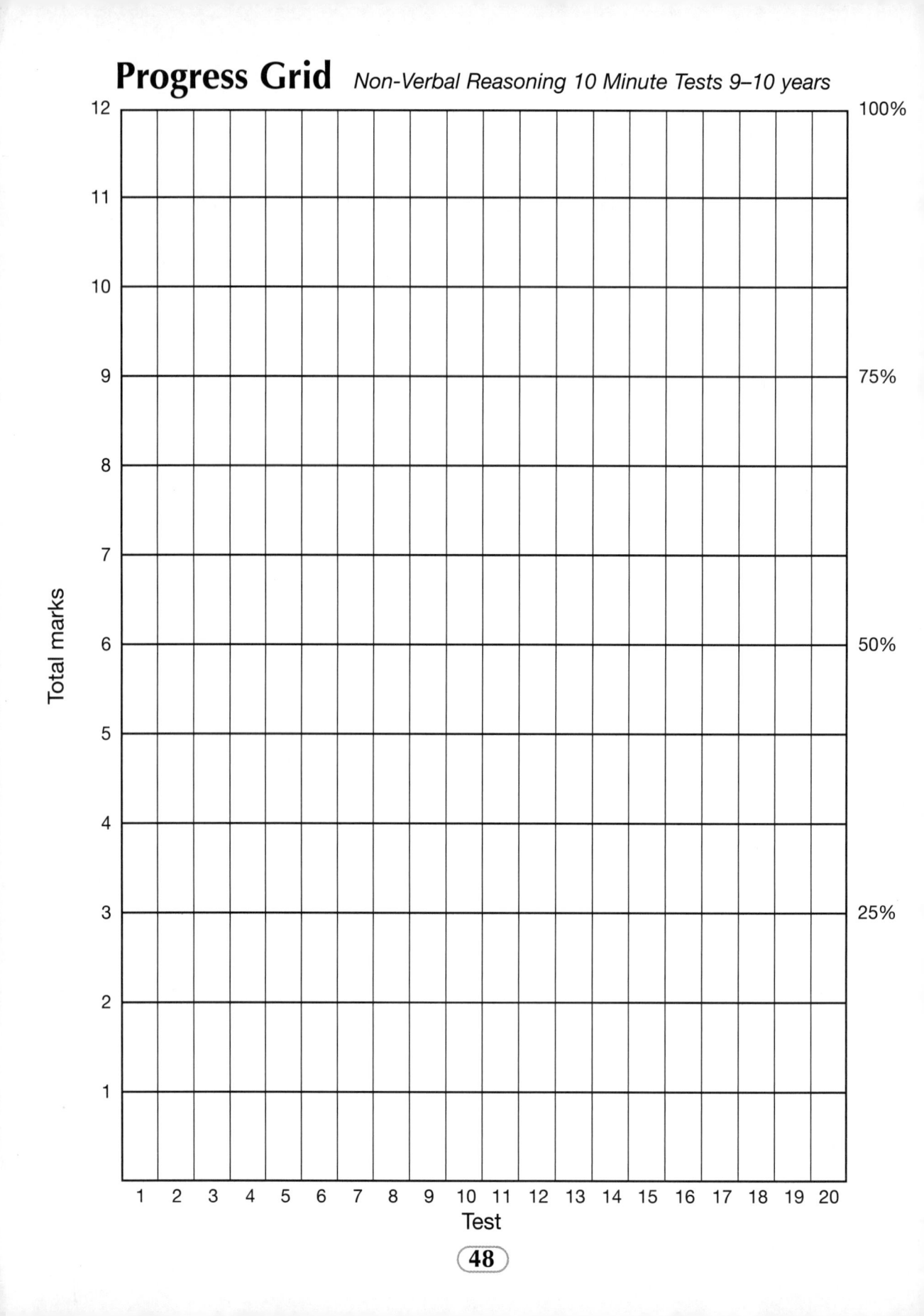

# Progress Grid
*Non-Verbal Reasoning 10 Minute Tests 9–10 years*

Total marks (y-axis): 1–12
Test (x-axis): 1–20

Percentage markers: 25%, 50%, 75%, 100%